C000303348

TO REPORT OR NOT TO REPORT

Survivor Testimony of the (In)Justice System

EDITED BY

EMILY JACOB

RESONANCE
PRESS

Copyright © 2018 Resonance Press
Cover Image "Mute Justice" Copyright © 2018 Lizzie Emmett

Foreword copyright © 2018 Emily Jacob
All testimonies are copyright © 2018 of the individual authors

The rights of the authors have been asserted in accordance with sections 77 and 78 of the Copyrights, Designs and Patents Act 1988.

All rights reserved. No part of this publication may be used, reproduced, distributed or transmitted in any form or by any means, without prior written permission except in the case of brief quotations embodied in critical articles or reviews.

For more information on any of our books,
visit https://www.resonancepress.com

Emily Jacob is the founder of ReConnected Life, a pioneering whole body/mind/self approach to recovery after rape. Find out more at https://reconnected.life

ISBN 978-1-9769-6753-5

FOREWORD

FOREWORD

This book started with a glass of wine.

It was an evening in March and I had been checking in with the women in my ReConnected Life Facebook Community, looking at their posts, providing support, checking they were supporting each other; reading. It was one of those nights which followed one of those days where it was so easy to get sucked into the void of hopelessness, of futility, of what is the *pointness*.

The stories of pain, and hurt, and betrayal, on this night, as they had been a lot at that time, were focused around the issues with the police, and reporting the crimes against us.

There were tales that haven't made it into this book, and tales that have. Tales of (what I would characterise as) gross incompetence: how could the video interview end up ruined beyond use in police recycling? How could someone be so injured, so obviously physically assaulted, but because there were no cameras working, the crime be NFA'd? (no further action).

I was angry. The so-called President of the United States had said he could grab us by the pussy, giving legitimacy to the entitled behaviour some men believe they have over our bodies. The Women's March had shone a crack of hope and solidarity and energy for a different world. And yet on the macro and micro levels, the President was still there, and my

Community were still feeling disempowered. Justice seemed a dream.

I don't like being angry. It's an emotion I don't handle very well. Usually I turn it inside on myself, the fists squeezing at my heart, in my chest, the inability to breathe, the tenseness turning to brittleness in my bones. Anger is so painful inside me, the tears leak. Instead of feeling strong by anger, as I expect those who display it externally do, I feel weak and fragile. And I don't like feeling weak or fragile. It makes me feel like a victim all over again.

And so, in the welling up of tears of fragility, buoyed on with the help of a few glasses of red wine, I decided to turn that anger into something positive, to turn that fear of feeling like a victim again into a warrioress' battle cry, and empower.

Our search for justice, for validation, is not heard, nor seen. The media only tends to report on stories that can be sensationalised: the celebrity trials, the rare false allegations. The *ordinariness* of the ordinary woman's search for justice is not newsworthy enough to be reported, and so the public perception is that rape is rare, because of course rape is serious and so would be reported. The experiences of the women who reported, who were told there was nothing to investigate, who were told there wasn't a winning case, who went to court but weren't allowed therapy until after, whose rapist went free. These stories are not told.

The de facto assumption when you disclose to someone, if they believe you (which isn't the de facto response by any means), is that you will report what happened, that justice will be done, and that means that the rapist will go to jail for a very long time.

That is simply not true.

As has been said (by Disraeli, and others since), there are lies, damn lies, and statistics. In the arena of rape, these statistics are at best murky to tie down to 'factual truth' due to the fact that as victims we are most likely not to report and so the crime against us does not get put into the system that collects the statistics; and at worst, spin-doctored to show agencies and authorities in as good a light as possible. It doesn't help either that many of the statistics for the UK are reported as England & Wales, Scotland being separate, and Northern Ireland too. Further, separating out child rape from adult rape is often blurred, and especially with the phenomenon of adult women reporting their rape from childhood. The statistics are difficult to pin down.

It's estimated that there are 85,000 rapes of women in the UK every year, but the Office of National Statistics (ONS) reported in 2015 that a third haven't told anyone of their assault. So actual numbers could even be much higher. The same 2015 report says that only 17% had reported the crime to the police. Of those, only in the region of 20% will get as far as court. And then there is only slightly more than fifty–fifty chance of conviction. If you were a rapist, you'd take great comfort in knowing the statistics were working in your favour. Improvements are being made, but shifting just a percentage point or two does not change the terrain. A light needs to be shone on the reality of what this thing called 'justice' is. Survivor voices must be heard, and heard with compassion and understanding.

Myths are widespread. The idea that reporting is an easy thing to do, that a wronged woman might just do that, and that that's a common thing and something for men to fear, is ludicrous.

It's far more likely that an adult man will be raped than falsely accused of rape. Yet the false allegations myth continues. All the men who are the subject of the rapes that are reported, but who are not prosecuted, or even if they are, if they are found not guilty, if their friends or family find out about the accusation, of course they will say they didn't do it. The myth of false accusations is perpetuated by those who got away.

In sharing these stories, my intention is to give those in the ReConnected Life Community a voice that can be heard.

In giving these survivor stories a voice, I hope to help others not feel so isolated in their experiences, to show how they are not alone and there is no shame in what they have endured, at the hands of the rapist, or the Criminal Justice System.

In sharing these stories of the lived survivor experience, I want to educate and encourage empathy and understanding in every single person working within and around the edges of the justice system: police, prosecutors, defence lawyers, the CPS, judges, juries. The presuppositions and preconceptions of victim blaming, which are rife throughout the System, need to be broken down, and this can only be achieved through a deeper understanding.

And finally, I wish to encourage an understanding and compassion of the survivor experience in the general public. Because until everyone realises that rape isn't rare but justice is, juries will continue to believe the myths that the rapist must be a monster and fail to convict the otherwise man 'of good character.'

My own story of reporting to the police isn't contained in the main body of this book. My summarised version is: I reported a month after it had happened. I believe the police believed me. Eventually, he was tracked down and questioned. Further on from that, I found out the CPS had decided not to prosecute; I was told at the time there was just too little evidence and it would come down to he-said/she-said. Two years later I found out the official reasons. They were:

- I had waited a month to report (this is very common, and I am so frustrated that this could be a reason not to prosecute at all!)
- I had been drinking (I was blacked out, drifting in and out of consciousness. I will never know if I had also been drugged and whilst I suspect I had been, from my own point of view of 'blame' or 'responsibility' I've done a lot of work on myself to know that regardless, I was drunk beyond the capability to consent. This should have been THE reason to prosecute and convict, because someone who is blacked out is has no capacity to consent to anything. It should have been an open and shut case of incapacity to consent).
- He offered into evidence photographs which he said proved consensual activity. I have never seen those photographs, and I know that they could not have shown consensual activity as I hadn't consented to anything. How can a photograph prove anything? This is the modus operandi of a rapist who wants to get away with it.

When I found out the reasons why the CPS had decided not to prosecute the man who raped me, I lost faith in the Criminal Justice System to provide on its promise of justice.

And that, for me, is a very personal betrayal of the system. My 'family business' is the law. My father has taught generations of lawyers to be lawyers. My uncle and my granddad have been High Court Judges. Grandad's knighthood coat of arms sits in my bathroom. The motto emblazoned on it, the family motto I grew up with, is Justice and Peace. I grew up thinking, believing, that with Justice, came Peace. That without Justice, there could be no Peace. I am grateful that my granddad never needed to know how deeply his profession had betrayed me, and that we never had to talk about how I could learn to embrace a world that did not include justice.

I am on the journey to making my peace with that world.

Peace and justice do not need to be tied together. As you'll see in the stories within, justice is not even a concept easily defined, and it's apparent that getting it does not mean that peace follows.

In editing this book, many of the authors' names, or identifying characteristics have been anonymised or amended. Some because they do not feel ready or able to 'out' themselves and waive their anonymity as a survivor of rape. Some because if they do not, they risk being accused of libelling their rapist as a rapist. Even in speaking out, we are so often silenced. The 'reputation' of the rapist is protected above our right to speak our truth and shed the shame that silence fosters. Silence hurts.

I know how hard it is to write your story. It can be cathartic, healing even. But it can also bring to the surface memories which have long since been forgotten, hidden, thought dealt with. I acknowledge the bravery and courage of all those who have found the words to put on paper. And all those who tried and found that they weren't yet ready.

This book is split into three parts. The first part is those who decided not to report to the police. Whilst statistically this is vast majority of those who are raped, part one does not reflect the majority of the book. This is not surprising; there is almost a further stigma to not reporting on top of the stigma of being raped. It is my hope that these stories go some way to explaining why it is such a big decision to go to the police. And when over 80% of rapists are known to the victim, it's hardly surprising that to 'grass' on someone you know, someone you might be related to, or need to work with, rarely happens.

The second part tells the stories of those who did report, and their experience of that process, whether the case was stopped at that stage, taken to court, or a verdict achieved. It is my hope that those reading gain a greater understanding for what it takes to go through this process. It can be a process that retraumatises. I am very aware that the reading of these stories may put some people off reporting, and in a world where the only way to catch a rapist is if a victim reports him, then that will not necessarily help improve the situation at a macro level. However, the decision to report is one that is the individual's choice, and that choice should be informed by an understanding of what it will involve.

The third part provides some thoughts and ideas from those who are supporting the victims of rape. They are speaking from their professional experience and expertise in working day in and day out to help victims navigate the justice system. I had wanted to also share the voices of those who work within the Criminal Justice System, as well as on the fringes of it. However, unfortunately none of my contacts felt able to. I do hope that this book opens up an opportunity for dialogue and conversation with those professionals. I am hugely grateful to those who did find the time to contribute. Without their involvement the risk was that this book was just a collection of moans at a system that doesn't work for survivors. I have been so inspired by hearing the work that these professionals are doing to both support survivors, and fix the broken justice system.

This book is dedicated to all survivors, everywhere. I pray you find your peace without justice, and live your ReConnected Life.

In solidarity and peace.
All the love, Emily Jacob xxx

GLOSSARY

- AVA (Against Violence & Abuse) - a leading UK charity committed to ending gender based violence and abuse
- C-PTSD - Complex post-traumatic stress disorder
- CJS - Criminal Justice System
- CPS - Criminal Prosecution Service
- IO - Investigating Officer
- ISVA - Independent Sexual Violence Advisor
- MPS - Metropolitan Police Service
- NFA - No Further Action
- OIC - Officer in Charge
- PCMH - Plea and Case Management Hearing
- PTSD - Post-traumatic stress disorder
- SARC - A Sexual Assault Referral Centre (SARC) provides services to victims/survivors of rape or sexual assault regardless of whether the survivor/victim chooses to report the offence to the police or not.
- SOIT Officer - Sexual Offences Investigative Trained Officer
- VIW - Vulnerable and Intimidated Witness

CONTENTS

DID NOT REPORT

SILENT SCREAMING
BY JUDE

I intend to tell my story and then explore the arguments I considered when deciding not to report.

My story begins around thirty years ago when I was seven and I lived with my mother in a small town near London. Money was tight, and mother took in lodgers to help make ends meet. When I was seven, the latest lodger moved in. He was the type of person that got on with everyone, great fun, reasonably intelligent and very sociable. He was also a chronic alcoholic with sociopathic tendencies.

As I was a shy introverted child, my mother saw the introduction of someone who could have fun with me and appeared to enjoy my company as a boon to the household. Coming from a repressed, not physically affectionate family herself, she thought it was nice that he was very tactile, hugging me, sitting me on his lap, giving me "big sloppy kisses that I hated" (quoted from a letter I received from my mother while on a school trip). My paternal grandfather was far less sanguine about this behaviour and mentioned his concerns to both my parents, neither of whom acted, but the warning did serve to keep the predator at bay while he knew he was being watched and I will always be overwhelmingly grateful to the nine years he bought me by his vigilance.

After a short period as a lodger, the man and my mother got

together despite the fact that they were ill-suited and frequently mean to each other. Even as a child I could see it was a toxic relationship and frequently advised each of them separately that they would be happier separating.

Around the time I was sixteen, three people died in quick succession. The first was my maternal grandfather, who died in the far-east with my mother in attendance who had gone out to nurse him. She came back a distraught, distressed version of herself. A few months later my paternal grandfather died and shortly after that my sixteen-year-old cousin. The ramifications of these deaths on my nuclear family were deep and far-reaching.

My mother, following the death of her father, had what in hindsight was a functional mental breakdown. To the outside world she seemed okay, went to work and provided for us, but she was deeply depressed and started having episodes where she would, not exactly try to kill herself as they weren't serious attempts, but she tried to hang herself from the curtain rail in her bedroom and the night before my eighteenth birthday she tried to gas herself in the car. I do feel a great deal of guilt for not realizing how serious it was and getting her some help. She also around this time started barring the door to her room at night by pushing a chest of drawers across it. With the clarity of hindsight this was to stop her boyfriend coming in when he got back late from the pub drunk and essentially raping her I suspect. She was also in a highly stressful job at the time and was at work for around twelve hours a day on weekdays.

I was more affected by the death of my paternal grandfather who I was very close to and my cousin who was a year younger than me when she died. I started self-harming and was very miserable. Her boyfriend used to take me down the pub with his friends and I found the fun atmosphere a welcome relief from the general miasma of sadness at home. Inevitably by the time I was sixteen I started drinking heavily at weekends and although I didn't sleep around I had the reputation as a party girl.

It was also around this time that the escalation in the lead-up to the rape began. My relationship with the lodger was emotionally and physically close, and the warning signs were all there. The first incident occurred one night when mother was asleep, and he and I had both been out separately drinking with friends. He came into my room, was sat on my bed talking and kissed me. He often kissed me on the lips, but this was a proper grown-up kiss. He left it at that and went off to bed. I felt very confused, but strange to say did not even consider the effect it might have on my mother—she was so distant emotionally and so often physically absent at the time that it was often like she didn't exist. Strange to say, but after this incident he didn't behave any differently towards me in the morning, as if nothing had happened. Perhaps he was too drunk to remember, I don't know and never will do.

There were other subsequent incidents, as well as his general behaviour which was unsuitable for a parental figure towards someone he called his daughter. Compliments about my body, references to what he would like to do to me if he was younger and instances where he touched me inappropriately. I never considered reporting any of these grooming instances as I naively didn't see that anything wrong was happening! With the limited experience of life I had at the time, the whole situation seemed normal, because I had nothing to compare it with.

The final incident occurred the night before Mothers' day 1998 when I was nineteen. I was just back from university for the Easter holidays and had been into town drinking, hoping to bump into friends but I hadn't found anyone and went home alone. The night had started with him and his friends in a different pub. I had one drink with them, kissed him goodbye on the lips as was 'normal' and then had a further two drinks in different pubs while looking for my friends. By my standards at the time it was a light night and I went to bed reasonably sober looking forward to a good night's sleep.

I awoke later in the night to find him raping me. There was no chance of preventing the assault as it was already happening. Bob Marley was playing on the stereo—Jammin'. I ought to explain at this point that as a member of the local TA he was in possession of, and knew how to use, a machete and an air rifle as well as various smaller knives. None were in evidence, but they were in the forefront of my mind as I frantically tried to make sense of the scenario. I wanted to survive, so I needed to be careful and not make things worse. My other thought was of my mentally ill mother in the next room. I knew it would destroy her to see what was happening, so I didn't scream, or call for help, or fight for both these reasons. I don't know if I would have been able to anyway, but I didn't try so will never know.

He had had a lot to drink, even by his standards. The unfortunate corollary of this for me was that he couldn't climax. And so it went on and on. Eventually even he realized it wasn't going to happen and decided to go down on me instead. At this point you might think it would have been easy to push him off me, but shock had set in by this point and my mind and body were frozen. After what seemed like an eternity he did leave. Bless beer, he'd drunk so much he needed to urinate and by the time he came back I'd regained enough control of myself to cajole him into going to bed to sleep it off. He kept asking for cuddles and it was a real strain to keep my voice light and unstrained so as not to provoke him. After he had gone I wrapped my arms around myself and lay in a foetal position, dry-eyed, numb. I didn't know what to do. The idea of calling the police never was a serious proposition for me at this point because of the two aforementioned reasons, my fear for my life and my mother.

The next morning, he was still out cold, so I took myself into the bathroom, locked the door for the first time ever and let the noise of the shower drown out my tears. I wasn't thinking of washing away evidence, I was just concentrating on trying to behave normally so my mother wouldn't notice anything. I remember crouching down in the shower, sobbing my heart out, desperately trying to make as little noise as possible.

The next day I waited until they were both occupied then left the house. I spent the next week homeless including one edifying night sleeping under a bush in the park. It was raining, and I don't recommend it! It felt safer than being somewhere I could be tracked down though.

In terms of the aftermath I was not thinking at all really, apart from in terms of getting through the next moment. A friend forced me to the doctors to get the morning after pill because of course he hadn't used protection and I will always remember the doctor giving me a lecture on safe sex. I replied twice that it wasn't my fault and eventually he must have taken this on board together with my unnatural stillness and asked if I wanted to involve the police. I shook my head and no more was said.

There were several factors which informed my decision not to report, two of which I have already mentioned: my fear of him and violence and my mother's wellbeing. I wasn't thinking of the evidence gathering but I thought that although I would probably be able to cope with a trial, she definitely would not.

It being 1998, there was certainly not anything like as much social media to consider and I was not an avid reader of newspapers at the time so felt no social pressure to report or not. My considerations were purely personal rather than thinking about society as a whole. I did consider that in my particular situation he was unlikely to attack someone else, and therefore didn't see that I had a duty to report to ensure the safety of other women. In years since I do have a paranoid fear that one day I will see something indicating that he has done, but so far, I've been lucky.

Another factor was alcohol. I'd had three pints of weak beer. Now this wasn't a lot for me, but I was aware it looked bad. As would my reputation as a drinker, good time party girl and the fact that I had kissed him on the lips in front of witnesses earlier that night. All circumstantial, but then most evidence in rape cases is, as sex is of course something which typically takes place without witnesses, be it consensual or not.

There was a further extenuating factor in my case—he had a friend in the local police. I didn't know his friend, and the friend was not a particularly close one of his, but I still had reason to be wary—I didn't feel I could be assured of the police's independence because of it.

Despite my reticence with officialdom I have generally been very open with friends and family about what happened. With some family members we have a tacit understanding not to talk about the incident which is fine. It is difficult because he was such a huge part of my childhood—effectively I cannot reminisce with family over pretty much anything that happened between the ages of seven and nineteen which is sometimes hard. Since my daughter was born there has been a lot of talk and photo evidence among my husband's family about whom she resembles. I have not been able to counter with anything from my side as all photos of my childhood have either been binned or hidden away.

Friends divide into three camps—those who have been one hundred per cent on my side, supporting me all the way; those who find the whole thing difficult to deal with and try and avoid mentioning it and a small minority who are no longer friends.

Oddly enough I get the same split of reactions from new friends as old. To be fair to the 'can't deal with it' group, they can be refreshing to spend time with as it gives a dose of normality and a respite from high emotion.

At the time I was only thinking of the talking side of the evidence, but I think I would have baulked anyway at the necessarily invasive evidence gathering. As it was it took me nearly ten years to pluck up the courage to have a smear and they still often result in me being unable to talk for some time afterwards.

The trial side of things I thought at the time I would be able to handle, but I have since reconsidered this rather blithe assurance after sitting as a juror on a child rape trial a few years ago. Even in this case, where because the victims were minors they gave evidence via video link and could not see the accused throughout, their distress on cross-examination was very affecting and the whole experience must have been very traumatic for them and the mother of one of the girls who gave evidence in court and was visibly very upset.

The experience of seeing other survivors going through the trial has backed up my feeling that not reporting, while not helping my recovery certainly didn't hinder it. Whereas I strongly suspect that reporting may actually have hindered it, simply because it would have kept everything current for much longer as well as placing restrictions on my movements—one of the most healing things I did in the aftermath was to leave the country for the back of beyond for around six months and then when I did return to the UK, it was to a different county without triggers from the last twelve years of my life round every other corner.

Although I do strongly doubt that my case would have resulted in a conviction, what did help me a great deal was when I found out that in the eyes of the law having sex with someone when they are asleep is statutory rape because they have not had the opportunity to give or withhold their consent. I found, and still find this very comforting because I know what happened and he was undoubtedly in the wrong. Proving it would have been another matter though.

I am also a believer in natural justice, sooner or later he will get his comeuppance. Apparently, it is going to be latter as the last I heard he was living a happy new life with a new girlfriend in Spain. But I still believe, and it brings me comfort.

In conclusion, although I have nothing against the police or the justice system in general, and I think they are a very necessary deterrent, in my circumstances I think my decision not to report was the correct thing to do. My best revenge is to live a good life—because he tried to destroy me but failed ultimately because I was too strong.

The message I would like to be taken from my story is that there are many reasons people cannot or will not report. I appreciate that for statistics' sake and where there is a case of endangering other women there is some sort of a duty to report, but a lot of people find the whole process too much at a time when they are distraught and feeling shut down anyway. Perhaps a useful service might be to have a process whereby people can report an incident has happened without necessarily taking it further or providing physical evidence. If there is such a mechanism in place I am unaware of it. I understand why the evidence has to be collected and how, but it is emotionally and physically abhorrent even when not in the middle of trauma.

The beacon of hope is that no-one has a 'normal' life—don't feel alone because you're not. Everyone has their own tragedy, some event in their life which represents personal demons to fight and conquer. The majority of people can manage to live a good life despite this—a life with friends and fun and happiness, so why not you? You are not to blame, stop blaming yourself and suddenly whatever the rest of the world thinks also ceases to matter which is incredibly liberating.

My dream of the future is of an accurate and accepted lie-detector. This would take away the need for cross-examination, physical evidence gathering and character assassination which puts a lot of people off reporting. It would also dissuade the women who make it so much more difficult for the rest of us by making false allegations. It might be a pipe dream, but so is anti-rape culture. Still. Twenty years on. Doesn't mean it couldn't happen someday though!

I will close with a song I wrote shortly after the incident which has given me strength over the years.

Screams in silence, non-ending pain
Will I ever be normal again?
Betrayal the first time, that I can forgive
The second I think not, disappearance forthwith.

He drank far too much, was he really a bad man?
But he forgets & I still remember, that I can't stand
So, leave me be, I long to grieve
For the loss of him I loved
A lament I believe
A lament he still breathes

Lament for a long time
Sing out the regret
For I wish what did, had not happened
We could play happy families yet

Screams in silence, non-ending pain
Someday I'll be normal again

TRAPPED IN A NIGHTMARE
BY ANONYMOUS

I was fifteen. I didn't know what consent was. I didn't know what sexual assault was. I didn't know I could say no. I was in a safe place—a local sport club I had been going to for approximately two years. We all knew each other, the teens were all cousins and friends, and on the other side of the hall were our parents, aunts and uncles. I was fifteen, he was seventeen. We were friends, I knew his cousins and we were in the same school. We had been out to the shop before, even went to the cinema together. I told him I didn't like him in the cinema and he stormed off, leaving me alone.

The club started again in September. My Mum would normally go with me but this day she didn't. We were both sitting at the side, talking. He asked me to follow him outside where he hugged me, and I hugged back. I remember feeling really uncomfortable, but he was holding me so tight and I didn't know I could scream no. He pushed me against the wall, put his hands down my top and kissed me. He was holding my wrists so tight there were marks the next day. I wiggled free and ran back into the hall with everyone else. I wanted to shout. As I looked around I saw everyone was part of his family and so I said nothing. I sat at the side the rest of the evening. At home I tried to scald myself in the shower, then covered myself in long clothes.

The next day in school I told my friend, she also confided her boyfriend was sexually abusive and her anorexia had returned. I watched her get help, everyone rallied around her. I tried to tell teachers as he would follow me around school, but I never felt close enough and what happened to me was mild compared with everyone else. About a month later I tried to tell my Mum what happened. She kept going on about how his name wasn't his real name. I wanted to scream at her to stop and listen, but she kept going on, only concerned about his name. She never noticed, if anything she was happy I stopped going to that club.

After Christmas I started cutting back on food, desperate to feel something, desperate for someone to ask if I was okay, to help me. No one noticed.

I was eighteen before I learned was consent was, after I was raped and abused repeatedly by another boyfriend. For three years I believed this was my fault. I still see him sometimes, now I can walk past with my head held high. Last I heard he had joined the police force.

I met him, when I was sixteen, and he was twenty-one. I thought he was strange but after seeing he was good friends with my friends and speaking to him, we became very close. Because of his age I felt I could go to him for advice, things I couldn't tell anyone else. When I broke up with a previous boyfriend he was there for me. He advised me to break up with him if I was so unhappy and true love could be closer than I thought. About a month later he asked me to go to birthday dinner with him. We had planned to meet up the Friday night before with a large group, but he couldn't as he said he couldn't afford it. I couldn't go out the Sunday as I had exams, but he assured me we could go out another day.

Another month passed before we actually met up and went out together. We went down to the coast and had a lovely evening. It was the first time I had been outside my hometown without family. I felt like I was on top of the world. We repeated this for a few weeks, each time he would say he cared about me so much and he was beginning to fall in love with me. We began to do things, but he would always go so slowly and ask if I was okay. I felt I had to keep going. I didn't know I had a choice.

Life got much harder, school became difficult and the homework never ending, learning to drive with an instructor who was unsupportive, arguments with my Dad every night—trying my hardest to ensure everyone was safe. With all this going on I didn't notice the mind games, I knew he was bad, but I had no idea how bad. He refused to see me for three months because I had a migraine, was so busy with everything else I never noticed it went on so long. Didn't notice the depression starting.

July was the first time we had sex, he promised he would use condoms but like all his promises it never happened. Three weeks later, Sunday before exam results were released—he raped me. I have never been as humiliated or scared before. I fell and banged my head. It was Wednesday before I realised what happened. Went to pick up exam results on Thursday—I did really well but I couldn't focus on anything other than the pain in my hips and dizziness in my head.

At this point I knew I had to get away, he would do worse again and I knew he was going to kill me.

My parents had always encouraged me to stay in school but now they started telling me to take the job, eventually I caved. My Mum completed the form for me in front of everyone and I had to sign it off. I was driven to my new work to give them the application the next day—it was a Tuesday. I felt so powerless, everything had been taken from me. I begged him to take me back after putting so much space between us, so I could leave safely. My parents became the new enemy. That night I couldn't cope anymore, I checked my bank balance and made a plan. I said goodbye to the only place I felt welcome—an Internet forum.

Three people responded. Two strangers and another woman I had spoken to a few times before. She stayed with me until 4am, until I fell asleep from exhaustion. She listened to me, she believed me, she told me what happened to her and it took her a year to get over it. She told me "sometimes being okay is the best revenge". I felt like she was the only person who truly cared.

Bumbling along, crying and sleeping I started losing a lot of weight. Instantly I had problems in work, I couldn't get along with anyone and I couldn't cope being surrounded by men. In November I started to realise what had happened, my period was late. By day three I was panicked, day five I was suicidal again. I couldn't have a baby to an abusive rapist boyfriend while barely able to look after myself. It's almost impossible to have an abortion here. Something told me to keep going, something told me to wait. On day seven my period finally arrived, I cried with joy but also, I was sad because this meant I had to continue living in the nightmare.

Soon after I realised I desperately needed help, professional help. I made an appointment to see my GP. But the GP had to cancel her appointment for the day, so the surgery called my Mum and told her that I specifically asked to see a female doctor. She texted me at work, I thought it was important so rang her back—she proceeded to scream at me and ended the call with "we'll talk about this later". I tried my best to hide the tears, but a few noticed and showed sympathy towards me. Later that evening when we were alone, it was quite late, and I was very tired she started asking what was wrong with me, before telling me there was nothing wrong. She asked if I had sex. I wanted to say yes it happened but no I didn't want it to happen. I wanted to say I need patience and love. I wanted to say I desperately need help as the next time I may not have anything to keep me going. I wanted to hug her, but I couldn't, I couldn't move. She just kept screaming.

A week or two later she took my phone while I was asleep and looked through it. I woke up early and couldn't find it, I couldn't sleep as I didn't know where my alarm was. I got up when I thought I should have, it was just before 5am (normally I'm up at 5:45am). She came down shouting about what she had read, that I was depressed and had sex outside of marriage (the ultimate sin according to her). She asked if I needed help and she would get me help if I needed it, she then threatened to tell everyone including my Dad who can be violent and hadn't spoke to me in months after a huge argument. Her offer of help was a threat, like I had let her down, let everyone down, I was pathetic. I really wanted to say I need my Mum, my kind caring Mum. I was afraid of the consequences if I did.

At the end of December, I tried again to get help, I contacted the Samaritans who were less than helpful. Onus and Women's Aid—both refused to give me any information and cited a refuge as the only option. Even though I explained I was suicidal and was not going to leave my younger siblings in danger. I was told by Women's Aid I didn't really want help or need it as I wasn't in immediate danger. Started having constant headaches so went back to doctors, saw three different doctors—none of whom believed an eighteen-year-old could have a constant headache or could be stressed. "It could be stress but you're a bit young for that". I will never forget her words, in those simple words she said what I was going through wasn't real. Nobody believed me I was depressed, no one believed me I was suicidal, nobody believed me I was in danger, nobody believed me I was trapped. When I walked into the room I felt the doctors judge me before I ever mentioned headaches or depression.

Since then I've found it extremely difficult to trust

professionals and ask for help when I'm ill. I went on and got myself out of the depression. As I got better he got worse and pretended to be dead. He threatened me not to tell anyone, he knew nobody believed me, so I would stop trying to get help. I was exhausted as he thought it was funny to pretend to be dead.

It would take a further two years before I was able to leave him. Immediately I found myself in another abusive relationship for a further ten months before I was strong enough to stand on my own two feet. This was when I learnt there is a SARC nearby, support groups ran by Women's Aid and sexual violence counselling.

I have never spoken to the police as in my area that's not safe. Very few people know my story, but I am ready to stand up and shout. I'm ready to break free of the final shackles of abuse.

PROCESSING TIME
BY JASMINE

I sat in a cold bath with sunshine lighting up the bathroom. The heat and the brightness of the day felt oppressive. I bumped into him at breakfast when my friends and I went out for the first day of 2016. He sat at our table and stared at me the whole time, sending me texts about how I looked tired as if we had in-joke to share about the night before. I felt sick. I went back to my apartment.

I was on the other side of the world to home, it all happened in a second language. It wasn't until my friend from home sent me a message saying I had to report it that I even considered the fact reporting was an option. She said it was my duty to protect other women from him. I already felt crushed by shame and self-blame, this comment about reporting, combined with my complete lack of faith in the justice system when it came to reporting rape, made me feel even more helpless.

I knew women with first-hand experience of rape and of the system back in the UK and to say the least, it wasn't encouraging. Then to be with none of my family or friends from home and with everything being in another language, the idea of reporting seemed entirely out of reach. But aside from these thoughts, the biggest thing holding me back was connecting with the idea that what had happened to me as "rape".

If you're going to go through a court case and official legal procedures, you have to feel relatively certain of your accusation. If you don't feel strong enough to call a spade a spade, then you will undoubtedly need to have support to lean on. Without this you will be alone, broken down by a legal system that will interrogate you as if you're the perpetrator. I regret that I neither felt strong enough, nor able to even begin to look for professional support.

At the time nobody at work knew, some of the colleagues and friends I'd got closest to in my time living abroad still don't know. I don't think I could have faced falling apart over there, so I tried my best to carry on as normal and faced the worst of my PTSD once back home in the UK six months later.

It actually took me two months to work up the courage to confront him, because I did in fact feel a sense of duty to other women. If I hadn't felt able to report it, I felt I had to do something pro-active to reduce the threat he posed. So I sent him a carefully constructed text message, detailing the ways in which he had violated my consent that night and how I sincerely hoped he would reflect on it and make sure not to do the same to any other women. I was very apologetic about having to break this news to him, as though I were responsible for any inconvenience he may suffer as a result of me bringing this up.

To my horror, his replies were full of anger. We exchanged texts for most of the day, until I gave up all hope of being able to make him understand his wrongs. I tried to give him a simple break down, educating him on consent. I used up a lot of energy considering how he might just really not get it and maybe if I patiently explained, he'd see the error of his ways and apologise for hurting me so much. This was wishful thinking. I've always seen the best in people but that day I lost some of my optimism and faith in others.

He said I just wanted someone to blame for my own regret of that night. According to him, I had wanted it, but was too closed minded about sex so made up a story to absolve myself of responsibility. He sent me about twenty pages worth of texts about how scandalous and ridiculous he found me, that I was clearly just a depressed person who needed a scapegoat for my own sadness and that if he had really sexually abused me it wouldn't have taken me 55 days to realise it. I thought maybe he was right and felt weaker than ever because if this was my entire fault and a choice I made then why was I so traumatised? Why did I feel like I was clinging on for dear life just to get by? That's not how a normal one-night stand was supposed to make you feel, was it?

His response made me feel stupid and filled me with self-doubt, even though every fibre of my body was screaming that what happened that night wasn't right. I don't think I could have handled having him say all of that in court with the backing of a lawyer and an audience of jury members, who could so easily be swayed by the misplaced but convincing confidence he had in himself. And that's if it ever even made it to court in this hypothetical scenario.

Looking back on it now I cannot believe my timid mouse approach in the way I spoke to him. My wording followed a tone a little like this, "um, excuse me? Sorry but erm, you need to have a bit more respect for women, maybe?" After seventeen months of processing, if today's me could go back, I would have screamed at him to get out the morning after. Failing that, I would have called him and said in no uncertain terms that what he did was not okay and then explained unapologetically all the ways it affected me.

The me now probably would have even tried to report it. I finally realise I did actually have a case. If I had been lucky enough to get a good police officer and a decent judge, he could well have been forced to face up to what he did. But the point is that victims of rape don't have seventeen months of processing time behind them when they have to make the decision of whether to report or not. Reporting only became an option in my head when I started to understand and accept that I had actually been a victim of a crime. By then, it was far too late.

There is no way the scared, vulnerable and weak version of me could have gone through with reporting it. There is no way I could have faced disapproving questions about what I was doing getting so drunk and why I let him into my house. Even now I feel like I have to highlight the fact he'd promised a friend to get me home safe after I'd been very sick and upset. I feel like I have to point out she specifically told him not to sleep with me in the state I was in and he assured her he just wanted to make sure I was okay.

The sad thing about this is I shouldn't need to defend myself even if I had welcomed him into my home with sober (or drunk), open arms. I'm already thinking in terms of someone who is trying to prove her case even though what happened should never have happened and nothing the victim does or doesn't do could change the fact their rapist chose not to get consent.

We are made to feel like we are the ones to blame and like we have to defend our own choices, all of which are seen to be a trail of breadcrumbs we leave behind on purpose, leading him to us as if we're "asking for it". It's like the more boxes you tick, "drunk", "short skirt", "kissed him", the more it's your fault if he ended up following the crumbs back to your body. Victim blaming, which rape survivors have to deal with for the rest of their lives, seems to crop up incredibly frequently and sometimes when you least expect it.

Recently I was on a retreat, hoping to get away from it all and focus on myself and my own wellbeing. I found myself in a group of women who were discussing a woman's blog post disclosing her rape at a yoga school in India. One of the women flippantly said, "I'd never let that happen" and "she should have gone to the police." It broke my heart to hear these comments, comments that I've almost come to expect from men but from other women? I couldn't believe the judgement that was being passed onto this woman for not reporting and the tone of accusation being thrust upon her.

This is another reason why I didn't report, because attitudes like this are prevalent worldwide across cultures. The idea that we "let it happen" and that smart women who follow the rule book of not getting raped end up safely unharmed for the rest of their lives.

When I first told the story I never ever said the words "I was raped", I just described the events of that night and how they unfolded and everyone else told me I was raped. I still struggle to use that word. I still have these niggling feelings of doubt that I'm not deserving of the support a rape victim should be entitled to.

I didn't actually *choose* to get black-out drunk. I'd been off alcohol for some time before and it took me by surprise, but even if I had decided to get completely off my face would that make it my fault some complete stranger decided to rape me? Of course not! It confuses me every day to see that so much of the conversation is centred around the victim and what they should or shouldn't have been doing rather than on the perpetrator and their decision to violate someone.

I have been made to feel as though I'm guilty for what happened, because I shouldn't have been drunk. A couple of close friends and family were quick to point out that I wouldn't have been an easy target if I hadn't been so drunk and that I had to address my behaviour. They seemed disappointed in me. Someone very close to me, who I've always looked up to, used the analogy of it being like him getting robbed walking into a dodgy neighbourhood with an expensive watch. Needless to say, this isn't helpful.

I can't change anything about that night now. Yet still, I've been berating myself from the day I woke up naked and confused with a strange man in my bed, sore between the legs with patchy memories of how I got that way. I don't know if I'll ever stop being angry and upset with myself for being so out of control of my own body. I mean, really, I should be angry and upset with him for taking advantage of a body that was so vulnerable and in need of care, but that's not how I've been wired to think.

There are many reasons I didn't report what happened to me. The biggest one being that I didn't truly feel it was my right to report. I was so worried that I was the one who had done something wrong. I didn't think I'd be taken seriously, but mostly I didn't know how to even put into words or categorise what had happened to me. It took so much time to peel back all the layers of self-blame, confusion, hurt and trauma that by the time I truly understood I had really been raped, I was back in England and reporting seems like it was never, and will never be an option.

Through all of this processing time, I understand a lot more about consent and feel more empowered about what is and isn't okay. I would like to think that reporting sexual assault is worth the fight and emotional turmoil but unfortunately, this remains to be seen. I hope with all my heart that reporting will become a more viable option for others, with a higher rate of conviction.

Luckily, I have had some very good support from friends and family. Even the ones whose first reaction was to comment on the fact I was drunk have since then, been good listeners and shown that they are there for me. It's a very complex and difficult process to know how best to support a loved one through something like this. The most useful types of phrases I have heard from my support network are actually very simple. It's things like "I'm here", "you're not alone", "you're safe" and "you're not to blame." I'm on a waiting list for counselling which I should be getting soon, and I feel stronger than I did this time last year. It does get better and I feel proud of what I've achieved since that awful night, even on the days where it's something as small as a single smile.

SERVING A KING

BY HANNAH GUEST

In 2012, I travelled to Africa where I spent four weeks working in a variety of healthcare facilities within some of the most deprived towns and cities. I had completed two out of the three years of my nursing degree and the opportunity had arisen to travel and experience healthcare in a different part of the world. I became aware of a company that specialised in facilitating overseas 'elective' placements for healthcare students. They arranged my accommodation and organised for me to spend time in one of the local hospitals. An optional 'add-on' to the placement was a week in a rural village, which offered the opportunity to live and work amongst a native tribe. I knew that this placement would be life-changing, but nothing could have prepared me for what I would experience.

I travelled to the village with another student, Rachel*. We were to live in a traditional mudhouse owned by a tribe leader called King Abasi*, who was employed by the electives company as a host and guide. The first day and night passed without incident, but on day two Abasi began to take advantage of me. Night set in early in the village, and with no lighting other than torches Abasi used this time to touch and kiss me. He told me that he was going to make me his wife, and that one day he and I would rule the village together. The abuse continued throughout the week. The village was a seven-hour bus ride from the nearest town and completely disconnected from all telecommunications, so escaping or calling for help was impossible. All of the power and control was his, and there was nothing that I could do but endure the abuse. At the end of the week Rachel and I travelled back to our accommodation in the city. Abasi travelled with us and dutifully ensured that we reached our destination safely. Turning my back on Abasi as I entered the shared house I believed that the nightmare was over. Unfortunately, the worst was yet to come.

After returning from the village Rachel and I decided that we would make one final trip into town as we were due to depart for our home countries the following day. After doing some last-minute souvenir shopping Rachel decided that she wanted to use the internet café. She told me to go back to our accommodation and assured me that she would follow later on. Several hours later she still hadn't returned, and I became increasingly concerned about her.

Then my phone rang. It was Rachel. Abasi had been watching us in town. When I had left he had kidnapped Rachel. For her to be safe I must go and join them. Without a moment's hesitation I called a taxi and rushed to Rachel's aid. Abasi's carefully orchestrated plan was in motion. Rachel and I were forced into taxis and taken to clubs and bars where other men were waiting for us. We were separated and taken to carparks, back yards and garden benches where we were made to pleasure the men in whatever way they desired. When all of Abasi's 'customers' had been served Rachel was allowed to leave.

I on the other hand had one more duty to fulfil. I found myself in another taxi, this time alone with Abasi. I was taken to a run-down, back-street hotel, where Abasi locked me in a room with him. Clearly he preferred a little more comfort and privacy to abuse his victims. Several hours into the ordeal I spotted an opportunity to escape. I fled the room, but Abasi was hot on my heels. I was forced into yet another taxi, but to my surprise this one took me back to my accommodation. When I thought about this later I realised, of course Abasi had to ensure that I returned to the house composed and seemingly unharmed, as if we had simply had an enjoyable evening together; to do otherwise would have raised suspicion. Later that day I packed my bags and boarded a flight back to England. I found a place in my brain to lock away all of the thoughts and memories relating to the abuse I had suffered, and vowed never to tell anyone what had happened to me. After all, who would believe me anyway?

Rachel and I initially responded very differently to our experiences. Rachel was fully aware of what had happened and the wrongness of it, and had the insight and reasoning to suggest that we could report what had happened to us to the in-country programme managers. In contrast, I had been subconsciously blocking out the abuse since it began (I would later learn that this dissociation was a coping strategy that I had developed in response to previous experiences). Nevertheless, Rachel's suggestion of reporting filled me with fear. What if we told the managers and they made us face Abasi, or what if he found out that we had 'told' and came looking for us? I was exhausted and homesick, and certainly not in a place where I was able to think or talk about what I had been through. All I could think about was getting home to my family and normality. I told Rachel that I needed some time to consider whether I wanted to tell anyone what had happened. She replied that we were 'in this together'. If we were going to report then we would do it together, if not then we would stand together in our silence. We had never met before we found ourselves on placement in Africa together, and came from different parts of the world, but we exchanged contact details and vowed to remain in touch.

For the first few months after I returned from Africa it was as if the abuse had never occurred. I shared stories and photographs from my trip with friends and family, including photos of the village and of my abuser, without even thinking about what had happened to me. It was as if my brain had erased all memories of the abuse. It hadn't, of course, it was just blocking them out.

About three months had passed when I started to remember the events from that week. The memories began to come back to me in the form of flashbacks and nightmares. I started having panic attacks and became extremely hypervigilant. I was on a community nursing placement at the time and found that going into people's homes was making me feel vulnerable and afraid. I felt very guilty for feeling this way; these were my patients, I was supposed to be caring, compassionate and professional towards them, but every time I went into someone's home all I felt was fear and an overwhelming urge to escape back outside. I was also beginning to struggle with my academic work— thoughts and images of the abuse were constantly at the forefront of my mind, forming a barrier to entry for any other information. These difficulties were being compounded by increasing fatigue as my sleep was punctuated by nightmares. I couldn't carry on like this.

I decided to make an appointment to see my personal tutor at university, with whom I had a good relationship. The enormity of the situation still hadn't hit me, I just thought "I'm struggling a bit here, I need some help". He noticed instantly from my body language that something was badly wrong. I wasn't able to find the words to tell him what had happened to me, all I managed was "something happened while I was on my elective... something that someone did". He asked me if I had been abused, and I nodded my head shamefully. His first concern was for me; he made an urgent referral to student support services and encouraged me to go and see my GP. However, we both knew that after what I had disclosed, some action would have to be taken to safeguard other students who may be at risk.

My tutor offered to contact the electives company on my behalf and inform them that he had become aware of an incident involving a student and a member of staff. He would gauge their reaction and ascertain the process for formally reporting the abuse. I agreed to this, and subsequently was advised to write a statement detailing the incident, for the attention of the head of the company. Before I began I contacted Rachel to inform her of what I was doing and to give her the opportunity to write a statement too. She replied that would be there to support me, but did not want to tell her own story, a decision that I completely respected. Then came the challenge of consciously thinking about all that had happened, such that I could put it into words in a logical order, and in a way that would make sense to someone who hadn't been there. This was more difficult than it sounds; trying to get my brain to do anything with the memories it held other than throw a selection of them back at me in the form of flashbacks was near impossible.

I figured out that the only way I could write out the sequence of events in the way I had been asked to, was to detach myself from them i.e. tell myself that this was just a story and that it hadn't happened to me. I adopted the role of a storyteller, a narrator. In my head I watched the abuse happening to my body, but I was not in my body, my mind was elsewhere. I finished writing my statement, but then I faced another challenge—allowing someone else to read it.

The thought of this story that I had written entering the hands of the company managers filled me with fear. It was only a few days ago that I had disclosed that I had been abused, now I was going down the pathway of formally reporting it. If Abasi's bosses approached him about it, he would know that I had told. What if he came looking for me? I knew that he had been to the UK before, and when I was with him in Africa he had talked about visiting again. However, I also knew that I had a moral duty to report what had happened to me so that action may be taken to prevent the same fate befalling other students.

I handed my statement to my tutor, who took it to the university's legal department. They recommended a few minor amendments, which I made, and then my tutor sent it on to the company. I was extremely grateful that he was acting as a go-between, as although I had decided to give my full name in my statement I think I would have been very fearful of liaising with the company directly.

A week or so passed before we heard back from the electives company; when we did, the response was not what we had hoped for. The company was questioning why I had waited until now to make a claim of abuse. They also reminded me of the positive evaluation I had given of my elective experience with them—I had even written a testimonial which had been published on their website. They clearly didn't believe me, and I completely understood why. They said that Abasi would be given a warning, but no further action would be taken unless other complaints were made.

I now felt a huge amount of guilt and responsibility. If Rachel and I had reported to the in-country managers before we departed, or even reported immediately after returning home, perhaps we would have been believed and an investigation launched, and/or more serious action taken against Abasi. As it was, Abasi would be allowed to continue in his role, with the potential that he could continue to abuse students. How many more people would have to experience what I had before he was caught? If only I had spoken out sooner, perhaps I could have prevented other students from suffering as I had.

On a slightly more positive note, telling my personal tutor that I had been abused on my elective meant that action could be taken to try to safeguard other students in the future. Students already received a series of preparatory sessions in the weeks and months ahead of their elective placements, but now an increased emphasis would be placed on safety. With my consent, students would be made aware that an incident had occurred, given advice about how to keep themselves safe, and instructed about what to do should anything untoward occur. I sincerely hoped that no other student had to go through what I had, but I prayed that if anyone else were to be abused by Abasi they would have the strength and courage to report it immediately so that action could be taken against him.

After reporting my abuse to the electives company my personal tutor fleetingly asked if I wanted to report to the police. I hadn't even considered this until now. I gave it some thought, but I didn't think that this would be a crime that the UK police would be willing to take on and I couldn't imagine the African police batting an eyelid at a report of sexual abuse— their culture attributes little respect to women and assaults are commonplace. I also had the company's reaction to my statement fresh in my mind, if they hadn't been willing to believe me and investigate then why would the police? I truly believed that the opportunity to report had now passed, that had Rachel and I told the in-country managers what Abasi had done to us before we departed then perhaps we would have been taken seriously, but now it was too late.

Another factor that contributed to my decision not to report to the police was that I didn't want to address what had happened to me anymore. I wanted to go back to my state of denial, where I was able to block out the abuse and continue as if it had never happened. I was in the final year of my nursing degree and until now had given complete commitment and dedication to my studies. I was on track to graduate with a First Class Honours and I was determined that nothing and no-one would prevent me from achieving this. I am very aware of how incredibly selfish this sounds, but I had given everything to achieve what I had so far and there was no way I was going to let Abasi take that away from me. I simply didn't have the time or the energy to put into a police report and subsequent investigation. I had heard how brutal sexual abuse trials could be for survivors—having to face their abuser in court and be cross-examined by the defence, and after all that the small chance of a conviction. Going through the courts would destroy me.

There was also the small matter that I had not yet told my family and friends what had happened to me, nor did I plan to. I had no choice but to deal with the pain and trauma of what I had been through, but I did not want to subject those whom I cared about to that—on the contrary, I wanted to protect them. If I reported the abuse to the police and an investigation was launched, I wouldn't be able to hide it any longer.

I am very glad that I decided to report my abuse to my personal tutor, and eternally grateful to him for the support that he gave me. My GP diagnosed me with post-traumatic stress disorder and commenced me on medication to help with my symptoms. I also received counselling from the university's student support services. I was given some time out from placements, granted extensions on assignments and allowed to sit my exams in a room on my own so that there were less stimuli to feed my hypervigilance. The university would ensure that other students were more safety conscious before going out on their electives as a result of what had happened to me. But despite all of this

I still carry a sense of guilt that I didn't speak out sooner and that I didn't report to the police.

I still think about Abasi and the village and I wonder if Abasi is continuing to take advantage of the students sent to stay with him. I do know that he is still in post, which means one of two things: he is still abusing students but they are either too afraid to report or report but are not believed, or; the warning he received after I reported to the company was enough of a deterrent to stop him from committing further abuse. I sincerely hope it is the latter.

NO WORDS

BY CLAIRE CRILLY

There are certain moments in each of our lives—snapshots in time—a feeling, a memory, a smell, that there are no words for. We can use comparisons, metaphors, similes; We can 'paint the picture', portray it through music, act it out, and yet still...it will not do that moment justice.

Some of those moments in my life, for example:
- Lingering along the sandy Tsavo Safari park in Africa, in a 'Jumanji-esque' style jeep, having dreamed of doing exactly that since as far back as I can remember.
- The first time I hurtled into a burning building when I graduated as a Firefighter.
- The moment I collapsed over the finish line of the Manchester Marathon to raise funds in memory of a friend who had died of cancer.
- The conversation which ended a seven-year relationship to follow my souls calling of travelling the world.

These are some of the indefinable positive moments of my early twenties. When I left the UK on 15 September 2014, aged twenty-seven, I was soon to learn the unfathomable negative moments for which I had no words.

I travelled to Sri Lanka, quite ironically, as a volunteer to help people who were living with trauma as a consequence of having survived the Tsunami and/or a civil war. I deliberately planned to start my solo travelling with an organisation, so I could quickly meet other people and have structure and safety whilst I got into the swing of backpacking. I believed it would be less daunting, less lonely. I wasn't disappointed. The twelve weeks I spent in the humming, swarming, humid streets of Colombo were life affirming, as were the weekends spent bus hopping to far throws of the Island. It was all I had dreamed of and I felt completely fulfilled; I had come home to myself.

The volunteering placement ended on 5 December 2014 and after several emotional goodbyes to my host family and new friends, I set out backpacking alone. Admittedly, I struggled more than I thought I would. There is certainly power in numbers and I missed the backup of my little team when I had to make decisions or motivate myself. It was hot, my rucksack was breaking my back, I had lost count of how many mosquito bites I had, and I STILL had head lice. I yearned for a cold, clean room where I could cook some healthy food, get a good sleep and recharge before flying to Australia on 19 December. Some research online (and subsequent internal bartering about whether I could justify the cost!) lead me to a Yoga studio on the south west of the Island. I had a four-poster double bed (and a quilt!), a highly powered air conditioning unit, my very own private kitchen next door (with teabags!) and running hot water. Another moment I struggled to find fitting words. Nirvana comes close. Early morning, I would do yoga with the other nine guests on the rooftop with the sea air weaving around my limbs. This was followed by afternoons reading on the beach, several catnaps and dips in the sea and then back for more sunset yoga. It was a very deserved and perfect ending to four months of hard work. Almost.

To celebrate my final night in Sri Lanka, I skipped across the road to the local beach bar where I had got to know the staff over the previous days when watching the sunset with cups of tea. However, tonight I was going to have a few drinks to salute this wonderful tear drop island. Yet twelve hours later, the tears and terror that gripped me as I regained consciousness and clambered out of a dark cellar room, were anything but a salute. My memory evaded me. My head was thick with whatever they had laced my drink with. I had been raped by a Sri Lankan man whom I trusted. After helping his people for twelve weeks. Again...no words.

It was 19 December 2014, 10.20am. My flight was leaving Colombo Airport in a matter of hours. I had to pack my rucksack and leave.

As the drug wore off, the reality hit and I wailed, in my plush room, with a fervour that I doubt and I hope will never grace me again. It was absolutely the most anguish I have ever known, and I trembled on the cold marble floor. I wanted my family, my friends, a hug. But I had to catch a flight, so as I rolled each item of clothing, so too did I roll my emotions and the events of last night into a tightly sealed ball. I was leaving this snapshot of time in Hikkaduwa and I would continue my trip as normal. All will be fine. I was a tough cookie.

Did it enter my head to report him? No

Not even a fleeting thought? No

I was incapable of that level of cognition. I was in shock and I was functioning on auto pilot and so I left a rapist in south west Sri Lanka to go about his normal life. It took almost eighteen months and several therapists to realise this action was holding me back from achieving acceptance and closure.

I often ask myself if I had of stayed in the country longer, would I have reported him? The answer is still no. Listening to the locals—and my attacker days before—I learned that the police were given a weekly sum of cash by bar owners to 'stay out of their business'. Additionally, in the months before going on my placement, I did some research and found damning reports on police brutality soon after the cessation of the Civil War. Admittedly, it was Singhalese and Tamil issues, however it did little for my faith in the authorities or the justice system. I made a silent promise to myself that I would be extra careful and avoid the police at all costs on my trip. Furthermore, I didn't speak the language. I was petrified. I was alone. I wanted out! And more than anything else, reporting it made it real. In the very early days—two–three weeks after the attack—I didn't view it as a rape; I viewed it as my stupidity for drinking alcohol and falling asleep. I had a new dark part of me, which I named the 'witch', who berated and tortured me for what 'I' had done. She ground me down to a shadow of my former self and I remained in denial, self-soothing with food, alcohol and cigarettes. That continued until I missed a period.

By a curious twist of fate, the first medical professional I saw in Australia was an older Sri Lankan lady. She treated me so gently and was apologetic on behalf of her people. I was upset by this as most of her people were lovely. It was not her place to apologise for one man's act. She did all the necessary tests, confirmed a clean bill of health and a negative pregnancy test followed by an offer of her going to the police on my behalf when she next went to Sri Lanka (two weeks later). This pierced me with a similar terror that I felt when I climbed out of that cellar. I truly believed they would hurt her or at a minimum, tell her I was lying and made it up. What proof was there? I was laden with shame so no...no. She could not utter those words out of this surgery. Or, imagine they did believe her? Then they would want to speak to me! Get a statement! What if it went to court? I couldn't bear the trauma of having to see a Sri Lankan man again, never mind being in a court room full of them! I was swiftly weaving my safety cocoon around me and I intended to stay in there.

When I began to disclose to a select few in the early part of 2015, almost every person's first question was "Did you report it?". Internally I was screaming "NO! WHY WOULD I REPORT IT? WHY WOULD I PUT MYSELF IN MORE DANGER? WHAT IF THEY DECIDED TO RAPE ME TOO? ARE YOU STUPID? DON'T YOU REALISE NOBODY CAN BE TRUSTED!"

It was only when I returned home to the UK in June 2015 (yes... I lasted five more months in Australia—I marvel!) that I felt truly safe and supported to start exploring the deep wounds that had been carved. A large part of this was dealing with how I let him 'off the hook'. I was haunted by thoughts and images of him doing the same to other travellers; destroying other girl's dreams. How could I not have reported him? Why is he not being held to account? I am now partly to blame for every other girl he attacks! And so the social media hunt began. I found him. Several of him flaunting and frolicking in that beach bar and I saved every last picture. I saved them to my home laptop, my work computer, my USB pen drive and I emailed them to each of my email addresses. I even printed them out. I now had tangible proof. I could do something. Justice would prevail. But how? How on earth could a shadow like me find strength to do ANYTHING which remotely felt like sufficient justice? I cannot make it clear enough—the light inside of me had gone off. I felt like the 'dead girl'. It was a momentous effort just to hold a basic conversation. It was impossible to make a decision or forward plan. It was terrifying to socialise, and every ounce of my energy was consumed with trying not to cry or fall into a ball on the floor. The best I could do at this time of my life was put one foot in front of the other, control my emotions and try to sleep. It was back to basics.

So I shelved it. But believe me... it doesn't go away.

It was almost two years on that I finally spoke about these pictures and started to uncover why I HAD TO have them and this unearthed a whole new depth of pain! Survivor's guilt a little? Cowardice somewhat? An enabler of him possibly? But mostly, I wanted justice. I wanted to believe that one day I would return to Sri Lanka and track him down and make him stand for what he did to me. Thus begun the process of acceptance that really...I was never going to do that. I wasn't going to stop a culture of drugging and raping in a foreign land single-handedly. Had I reported him, would closure have come sooner? I don't think so because I believed, and still do believe, nothing would have been done.

But it doesn't make it right. A dodgy justice system should not be the reason that such a catastrophic and damaging event in my life has gone, for the most part, unnoticed. Undocumented. Unmeasurable. Unspoken. Which is the reason I am writing this. Silence is not good enough. If you report or if you do not report, just do not let it be in vain. Put the effort into healing yourself and when you feel strong enough, use your voice! Use your story! Our society needs to hear the true side of rape and its consequences rather than summarising our experiences based on tabloid headlines.

I am proud to be a survivor and I am proud of everyone who has helped get me here.

DID I DESERVE THIS?
BY ELIZABETH MONCRIEFF

One Sunday in September I was at a party. I was drunk. So drunk that I barely remember the latter part of the evening or going up to bed, only flashes of consciousness here and there. By some people's standards that would mean that I brought this on myself. That I knew of the dangers when I swallowed drink after drink after drink. Some people would say that I even asked for what happened to me by letting myself get that drunk. Would it change your mind if I told you the party was at my own house? It was my mum's birthday party, get-together, gathering, whatever you want to call it. Would it change your mind if I told you that I was in my own bed when it happened or that the only men attending the party were my brothers? Did I still deserve it?

It was fear that stopped me from reporting my rape. Fear and denial.

When I woke up the morning after I was (maybe) still drunk and confused but had to get up for work so I just carried on as per usual. I thought the small flash of consciousness when everything was over, and I was pushing my brother out of my bed was some kind of messed up dream because there's no way that he would have done anything like that, right?!

I clung so tightly onto my denial that I just carried on with life as usual, completely ignoring what had happened until a couple of weeks later when my period was late. I still couldn't admit to myself what had happened, not completely, because admitting to myself what had happened did not help me in the slightest. Knowing whether or not I was pregnant was at the top of my list...then when the test turned positive I broke down. I hadn't been sexually active since I broke up with my partner at the beginning of the year, yet here I was in October, still unable to admit to myself that my brother raped me and now I was pregnant. I made an appointment with my doctor to be referred for an abortion, something I thought I would never have to do. That doctor was the first person I told about what had happened to me.

I went through with the abortion and, because I had told the Marie Stopes nurses how I fell pregnant and why I needed an abortion, they were duty bound to inform the police. The police made first contact with me; I know that this is unusual. So I didn't actually report my rape, but I was still talking to the police.

The officer on the phone seemed understanding and was urging me to allow the police to carry out an investigation. I couldn't let them do it. The officer wanted to come around to my house to talk to me about it before I made the decision about reporting or not, but I lived with my mum at the time and she didn't know. I couldn't have the police at my house. So I told him no. I wouldn't even give him my brother's name. There was an element of protecting my brother by not letting them investigate but I was mostly scared.

Scared of what was to come if I was to go through with reporting it, after all, according to some, I deserved what happened to me. I couldn't bear to be questioned over and over about something that I hadn't even shared with my closest friends or family.

I was in counselling at the time for an unrelated issue and I hadn't even told my counsellor what had happened until after the abortion and the phone call from the police.

I was ashamed. Could I have somehow caused this?

I couldn't bear being questioned over and over about a situation that I hadn't even admitted to myself fully. Questioning doesn't mean that you're believed. There would have to be proof involved somewhere, actual physical proof but I had none of that. I was told as much when the abortion process started, that all physical evidence will be lost with the developing foetus. Every girl knows that if you're raped you do not clean the clothes you were wearing at the time, but I hadn't even admitted to myself that I was raped until weeks after, so it was safe to say any physical evidence had gone down the drain or the toilet.

I was scared of being asked whether I thought there was anything I could have done to deserve this because according to popular opinion I had let myself get to a point of intoxication where I made myself vulnerable; therefore yes, I did do something to make myself more deserving of this horrendous act. I was fearful of how I would be treated by the police, mainly because of the few stories I had read in magazines. I was scared that they'd ask me about my sexual history, because I felt like my less than prudent past would be used against me. That all the one-time partners whose names and faces I couldn't single out in out a crowd would somehow be used to tell me that I deserved it. I didn't need anyone else telling me something I had already told myself more times than I can count.

Because in the eyes of the media, I deserved it. The rhetoric in the press these days is one of 'victim blaming'. This is a term you hear thrown around so candidly that the MEANING behind what it implies has been lost. So I ask of you to actually consider what it is to suddenly become one of those victims that you have previously only read about. To me, it meant that I must somehow have been asking for it. That the responsibility of what happen to me whist I was asleep in my own home, my own bed, lay firmly on my shoulders because I dared to make myself vulnerable. I dared to believe that I was safe therefore I am to blame.

I guess another reason why I didn't report was because I knew the man who did this to me. I loved him, he was one of my closest friends, and he was my brother. We had grown up together and he is a gentle and kind man. He is a man that has a problem with drinking but here is not the place to argue the about the horrors that alcohol brings to millions of families each year. My point is I knew this man, I would go as far as to say he was the only man I trusted after being abandoned and mistreated in the past (read daddy issues and a string of bad relationships), but when this happened, when I could finally admit to myself what had happened, I couldn't bear the thought of talking to complete strangers about him. I couldn't bear to hear his name and the word 'rapist' in the same sentence.

It's a common misconception that rapists are strangers in dark alleyways late at night waiting to pounce. That is a complete myth but during the following weeks of abortion clinics, faceless nurses and police officers, I still could not admit to myself that I had been raped. That sounds mad to me now but at the time that myth of what rape is, of how women and men are raped was screaming so loud in my head I was silenced. In a world where you need a cartoon about cups of tea to clarify the concept of consent I did not think I had the right to report this. Even though I knew that I didn't want that to happen to me. Even though I knew that it was incest. It was wrong. Even though nurses were telling me do so. Even though the police got in contact with me. I still didn't feel like this was the correct type of rape or I was the correct type of victim. I guess it comes down to blame. I have only just started to internalise the fact that I am not to blame for any of this.

I blamed myself to the point where I didn't believe there was a crime to report.

Despite all of this I have had moments where I regretted not reporting it, at times all I wanted was to see him punished in some way because it seemed like the only person being punished for his stupidity was me.

During these times though I suppose I didn't trust the 'criminal justice' system was able to provide that punishment. I kept on thinking of the time I was mugged. I had my phone stolen from my hand on a bus in London where my muggers were seen clearly on CCTV. Nothing ever happened to those two boys who stole my phone. I was lectured by police to no end about how I just shouldn't have my phone out on the bus. I could not fathom a way in which the same 'criminal justice' system could offer any such result from a case with less evidence. Also, I had already beaten myself up for getting blackout drunk on that night; I didn't need another lecture.

It took me the best part of two months to tell my counsellor what had happened to me (I had already been in counselling for six months before my rape) and a further three months to tell any of my family. I have never experienced so much support. and I feel that it has been because of their support that I have been able to process what has happened to me and begin to move past this, as much as you can. I guess what has got me through this situation is that continuing support, and the fact that I am lucky enough to be able to fund my own mental health care so I am not at the mercy of lengthy wait lists. I felt nothing by fear when I thought of reporting this to the police, fear of judgement and hostile treatment by the people who are meant to protect his country. It was irrational fear as I didn't have first-hand experience of the rape reporting process but I was still scared.

I felt like my rape didn't matter because I had somehow

brought this upon myself so therefore I wasn't worth protecting. Those kinds of thoughts are like poison and serve no purpose but to further blame the victim. Reporting anything (from a mugging to a rape) is hard emotional work. It is repeating the trauma over and over again in a room filled with strangers treating you with suspicion.

I wish someone had told me when I was struggling that there is no shame in not reporting. That the act of not reporting does not make you any less deserving of love and support. So, if reporting does not feel right for you, that is okay.

Reported or not, I would urge everyone who has survived sexual assault to speak to someone, anyone who you can trust. A problem shared is a problem halved as they say and, although sharing your story will not make the pain go away, it will ease some of it. Shame can weigh us down until we feel like we're wading through tar. Confide in someone, and if anyone ever tries to tell you it was your fault because you were drunk, you led them on, you dared to wear a short skirt, or anything besides 'you are not to blame' they are not the ones to share this with. Because when you are going through this you need people who will build you up not try to kick you while you're down.

We need to work to create a system where anyone who reports that they have been raped is treated with sensitivity not suspicion. To actually have organisations who want to genuinely help these men and women who have had their sense of security ripped out from underneath them. To move away from this rhetoric which assumes that someone asked for this to happen because that could not be further away from the truth if it tried. We need to move towards a system that wants to deliver genuine justice, not just a slap on the wrist.

The reporting process is surrounded by so many myths which only serves to increase the fear felt by survivors and to further silence us. There needs to be some transparency instead of this urban legend style perception that is reported in the media. We need the have basic compassion for those who are at a vulnerable time in their lives, to offer understanding not suspicion.

DID REPORT

NO-TELLING

BY RAIN MARTIN

I decided not to report, at first. I was too scared, intimidated, and overwhelmed. However, several months down the line, I found both the tenacity and courage to go report him. I had been taken to hospital on the night of the rape, so there was medical testimony on file. The bruising and injury could not be argued other than from the attack.

But, I was called to the District Attorney's office sometime after I reported the incident to the Police, where there were at least three State Attorneys present. They were all men. They told me that they will not proceed with prosecuting charges against the perpetrator—they thought "it would be too traumatic for me" owing to the fact that he could use various arguments against me. Instead, they recommended that I take the event of the rape to the University Disciplinary Body, where we were both then registered. They suggested I go for counsel with legal aid, which I did.

The Legal Aid Clinic assisted me in providing the information needed for the University Disciplinary Committee. However, both he and I were in our final year at the University, so the University delayed the disciplinary hearing until early the following year... at which time neither he nor I were any longer registered for study, having completed our degrees, and making the disciplinary process redundant. I was told "to move on with my life, and not let this affect me".

All very convenient for the University who no longer needed to address the issue in a confrontational manner; devastating for myself, who felt betrayed by the lack of follow-through on all scores by both the State and my Alma Mater. I felt that "The System" fundamentally protected him (the perpetrator) versus me, and that the ordeal I had to go through to report the rape (not to mention the intrusive hospital process in order to get medical care in the first place) was beyond my capacity to endure.

All the words that had to emerge from my mouth at the time of reporting, were as terrible to say aloud as I had imagined it would be... After I had explained what happened, the police required me to state word for word, explicit details on what exactly occurred during the rape. This was necessary for them to draft the affidavit. "I nearly died" is an understatement—a piece of me shrivelled up deep inside and never re-emerged.

What was a brutal rape, and harmful attack on me physically by someone known to me, also became a more devastating process in its aftermath. His friends that were fellow students ganged up to "protect" him, and would publicly approach me on the matter, surrounding me. It was crushing and traumatic. I felt that everyone knew who I was, and that I had been stigmatized.

Furthermore, there was a time during the reporting phase when I would repeatedly find my vehicle with its tyres slashed, the wheels flat and un-drivable... all tremendously costly and unaffordable for a student, but besides that, utterly terrifying to my psyche.

I survived, but the price was immeasurable. My sanity hung by a thread, and I felt a scourge on my dignity. To this day, I never disclosed to my family that I reported the rape, as they were against me doing so from the onset; they wanted me to carry on as though nothing had ever happened. I felt that they would never be any support, if anything they would only condemn me for taking action (versus silence) and exacerbate the shame I already felt to be immense.

FINDING MY VOICE
BY ALICE COUDÈNE

I remember the day I decided to report. It was, and still is, one of the biggest decisions of my whole life. Maybe THE biggest decision.

It was on my birthday. Could it be more symbolic? Like a rebirth, 6 years, 5 months and 162 days after the facts. It was not an easy decision, but I was ready and above all I had the capacity to do it.

I could not report when it happened. It can sound strange for anyone who has not been in such a situation. *"Why did she not report?"* is one of the most common questions we get when people start to comment about rape stories. And it is also one of the most guilt-inducing.

It seems logical to report a crime. Unfortunately, logic does not always work and is not always applicable depending on the situation.

In my case, many reasons prevented me from reporting immediately and I think it is important to have a focus on those reasons in order to understand why.

I was totally incapable to react, and I lost my voice for almost a day after the event. I was so in shock that I still do not know how to describe the state I was in.

It was the first time I was raped (according to the law) but not the first time I was sexually and physically assaulted.

Everything happened in France. The first time I was ten. It happened in a public space with other children and adults all around. It lasted two years. I was repeatedly assaulted and humiliated. Once it included a knife.

No one intervened. I was terrified. I knew something was wrong and I was hoping that someone would say something, do something to help me to get out of this nightmare but no one intervened. Never. So, I started to think and believe that what they were doing to me was normal because if not, why did none of the adults around intervene? Why did some people even call this a "child's game"? I know nothing more disturbing and confusing, especially as a child. I tried to speak up, to seek help a few times at the beginning but the adults did not listen to me. They did not even hear me. I was told to get thicker skin and to shut up because they did not want me to create problems where there was none. Boys will be boys after all.

My abusers found it so funny. Like a good game indeed. And I inspired in them a lot of jokes. Rape jokes. Me, being sexually assaulted, tortured at knife point is a joke. Jokes are only harmless fun, right?

I was a child, abused, silenced and told that what happened was nothing but instead something laughable and not serious.

This taught me that I was nothing, my body was nothing but public entertainment and that boys may grab and hurt me as much as they wanted.

Besides that, I could watch and read every single day facts and stories that made me feel very bad but that were romanticised, glamorised or lessened almost every time I switched on the TV or opened a newspaper. I remember clearly reading and hearing words such as "seducer" to qualify an alleged or convicted rapist, "forced into sexual relationship" and even "making love by force" for what was, in fact, rape. The concept of the "French lover", "la drague" (what we call now street harassment) was (and still is) so ingrained that being catcalled, whistled, followed, stalked was/is the best compliment ever.

So, when this guy harassed me in the street, followed me everywhere for hours and eventually raped me I could not react. I told him I was not interested, I did not want to talk to him, I was in a hurry and to leave me alone, but he did not care at all and, once again, I saw some bystanders laughing at the situation. I could not find any escape. I was not only telling "NO" to him but also to all bystanders who contributed to create the hostile environment for me and a free game zone for him. I froze and disassociated during the assault. When I reconnected, my voice had disappeared. I was blocked and acted like a robot. I could not even name what happened. I could not find the word "rape" but had in mind the "child's game" the "good joke", "seducer", "compliment". I was totally lost. My feelings, my reality did not match with the words that popped up. Could I really go to the police, telling them I was in so much pain that I thought I was going to die because I met a seducer who complimented me by having a sexual relationship of forced love with me? I really considered my rape this way.

Could I even tell I was completely dissociated? We know more about freeze and traumatic dissociation now, but it is not a mainstream topic either. It was even less at the time I was assaulted. I did not understand my reaction.

I was the problem.

It took years for me to understand that the problem was not me, that it was not my fault, that I should not feel guilty.

It has been a very long and painful path to realise I was not the one to blame. Then, I could start my recovery process. I got the opportunity to move abroad as an exchange student. It helped me so much.

Discovering a new country and new languages changed my

life. I was not in my daily routine anymore. Everything was new. I could start from zero.

I had to express myself in two new languages, in English and in the official language of the country. Speaking other languages helped me to get some distance with the brutality of the words. "Rape" does not sound like "viol" and the sound of "viol" was terribly triggering.

Little by little, I got more confident, stronger and able to use the real words for what happened. It became clear that I never did anything wrong and therefore I deserved peace and deserved to live a good life. My life. I deserved to transfer the burden of the assaults onto the perpetrators. I had to report. It was crucial for me because it was a way to turn my shameful rape into a crime for which the only person to be held accountable is the perpetrator. A crime like any other. I wanted to be recognized as a victim of a crime. It was important for me to get this recognition because it would mean that what I had been through was wrong and reprehensible. I had been victim of the crime of rape.

I would like to say a word about the term of "victim" because it could be misunderstood. I use it as a legal term to describe a legal situation. I was raped. Therefore, I was a rape victim. This does not mean that I should be victimised. I should not. This does not mean I am a poor defenceless victim forever. I am not. I do not wear a mention on my forehead "rape victim". What happened to me does not define me. My choices define me, not something I did not consent to.

So, I decided to report.

The law is quite complicated. I wanted to know if it was possible to report the attacks I suffered as a child as well. The delay to report a crime is ten years from the facts if you are over eighteen-years-old or twenty years from the age of majority if the facts occurred as underage. So, in case of rape as underage you have until the age of thirty-eight to report.

The problem in my case was to know if the assaults were legally rapes or "just" sexual assaults. If rape is a crime, all others kind of sexual assaults are offences. The delay to report an offence is much shorter and I was not sure I was on time to report.

Another issue was what should I report? Should I report every assault? Should I report the whole period? It lasted two years.

I had to consider the fact that the perpetrators were all underage as well and therefore not submitted to some charges. Then, should I report against all the adults who witnessed the assaults?

It was quite difficult to gather information and it was emotionally excruciating. So, I decided to report the street harassment rape case only.

I did not know how to do it. I Googled a lot and found some organisations to contact. I called one who gave me some legal information and good advice. They warned me about a "decriminalisation", almost systematic, in case of prosecution and trial. One of the arguments is that a trial for crime is tough for the victim, a decriminalisation implies less toughness and there is a bigger chance of conviction.

I knew I had a very tiny little chance to go to a trial as I did not know where my rapist was, but I knew that if he could be caught and prosecuted I would go to the court and refuse a decriminalisation if I had the right to. Rape is a crime. It destroyed years of my life. I will not let anyone lessen it into a simple offence.

I got prepared for the police report. It was, indeed, what I most feared. I knew they could ask me intimate and sensitive questions, especially because I reported years after. I expected to be asked to justify why now and not before.

I prepared myself for the worst and organised everything. I booked my flight tickets, a hotel, asked for some days off at work and made a list of all the organisations in this region of France that could help me during the process.

Nothing went like I expected and what I feared the most appeared to be the easiest.

I was very nervous when I arrived at the police station.

I told the reception why I was there, and a man came to pick me up for the report. I thought he would take the report, but he left me with a female officer. I was ready to speak with a man, but I felt better speaking with a woman. She made me feel comfortable, apologising for some questions like *What were you wearing*", she listened to me but what I will never ever forget are these three words she said to me:

"We believe you".

That was all I needed.

When I went out, I felt strong, confident, brave, empowered.

It did not last.

Soon after I went to a women's organisation, hoping to gather some more tips and legal advice. I ended up behind a closed door alone with a man bombarding me with humiliating and irrelevant questions. He even asked me why I did not want to have sex with the rapist. He told me to lessen it into an offence. He also said that if I did not have sufficient proof I would be condemned for defamation and this is a very good thing, according to him, because we can't accuse people just like that.

Like what???

I was numb when I left.

Then, my boss sent me an email saying not to bother to come back to work. I was fired. I was giving a bad impression.

It had cost me years to find the strength to report, and everything collapsed. She was clearly punishing me for speaking up and reporting a crime. She did not let me go back to pick up my stuff. The case was not even about someone in the company (and even if it had been someone in the company it would not have been a reason to fire me). All the progress I had made in years were swept away. I remained silent for years again. I was terrified that somebody at work could find out I was raped and fire me again.

I was devastated but I kept in mind the words of the policewoman "we believe you" and I could count on very good friends. Then the internet and social media provided me a great help thanks to some Tumblr, blog and pages. At last, I could read words from others, victims and survivors.

I moved soon after the report. I went back for few months to France before I moved to Spain. Once again, learning a new language helped me to re-appropriate my words and my story and I found a wonderful association in Barcelona that provides great help. I am not ashamed anymore and I will not remain silent. If anyone rejects me for being raped, he or she does not deserve my time, my interest and even less my friendship. I am not afraid anymore to be alone. I am not alone. This collective book is a proof. We support each other. We have a voice. Writing is a voice too.

My case never went to court. They never found him. For me, now, this is a closed case. On a legal level.

Now I want to live a normal life, free of the PTSD I developed due to the assaults and enjoy it as best as I can.

I want to claim my body, my life and my right to feel free and safe in the public space. I started a personal Instagram project about that.

I am willing to speak up as much as possible and I am involved in various projects to tackle sexual violence. One of them, "Nuestras vidas como denuncia. Historia de no ficción" is a documentary project about denunciation and representation of women and sexual violence in movies and media lead by a group of young women filmmakers. I am currently making a short movie as a part of it. This violence is not a fatality. We can fight it and win. I believe some measures could change a lot this issue. I have concrete ideas like:

I wish informational training would be given for all journalists who write about sexual violence issues and cases. Newspapers and TV, web magazines etc… inform us every day about what happens in the world and they have a great power and responsibility by presenting the information to their public. We learn the information from them.

I do not think you can pretend to cover a sports event because you have seen a movie about this sport if you do not even know how many players are required to make the team. Then, why could you pretend to cover a sex crime if you know nothing about this kind of violence, its consequences, the sequels it can produce? Just because you saw it on a TV series made by people who do not know anything about either?

I, for example, am involved in a project in Barcelona "Dones Valentes" lead by journalist and co-director of Master de Genere Isabel Muntané in collaboration with AADAS, an organisation that provides support and services to women and children victims of sexual violence. The project won a 25N special price from the city of Barcelona. The aim is to organise meetings between rape victims and journalists in order to start a conversation on why some words, some structures of phrase can really hurt and have a huge negative impact.

What I read in the newspapers influenced me not to report. The "seducer", the "love by force…" I read it and I was so confused and devastated. Now with this project I met other victims who have been and still are affected like me. I want this to stop. We want this to stop. And who knows better than us how it feels, what it implies, what the difficulties we meet are, how we can recover, how we can live (and can be happy as well)? We experienced it in our body, in our soul, in our flesh. We know. So, please ask us and listen to us.

I wish there would be good sex education at school with a focus on consent and respect and an introduction to what is sexual violence and an explanation of what is PTSD, traumatic disassociation and all the traumatic responses. There are more than just flight or fight. There are also freeze (it is what happened to me), submit or attach.

I wish children would be taught with some adapted words and activities that no-one is entitled to their body but themselves.

I wish every single person who is willing to fight against sexual violence would ask her/himself what he/she can do if witnessing a case of violence or a depreciation of violence like victim shaming or rape joke. I have never met any rape victim laughing at a rape joke (except nervous laugh as a physiological strategy to avoid a panic attack and flashback like it happened to me and many others). Honestly, what is funny about a crime that can have the same consequences than torture, that is considered as war crime when committed in a war zone and that is so frequent that you are surrounded by victims every day? It is a mathematical certainty. We are surrounded by people who suffered sexual violence. Maybe rapists will laugh and understand what is so funny. But all the others? The majority who are not rapists? Please stop. We are not making jokes about stolen mobile phones. I am pretty sure such jokes exist but so far no one told me any stolen mobile jokes (my mobile has been stolen twice in my whole life), but people were/are telling me rape jokes. (I can't even count how many assaults I endured). Yet, losing my mobile this way did not induce me PTSD and years of recovery.

I urge everyone who is able to speak up safely to do so.

May I dream of the harmonisation and simplification of the legislation? At least at the EU level? And a better system for people living abroad. It cost me money and time and energy to go back to France to report. I first thought it would be possible to report at the Embassy but apparently it was not. I was lucky enough I could afford it, but I am afraid not everyone could have. Being able to report from a foreign country would have been a relief.

There should be no time limit for rape and sexual assault. We must be allowed to report when we are ready to do so.

I believe that with better coverage of cases of sexual violence and with better education we can reduce the rate of this violence and reassure the victims that they are not to blame but are allowed to speak up and be listened to.

If only one of the adults who witnessed my first assault could have stopped these three 11-year-old boys who touched me and told them that they could not do that instead of looking away or laughing at the incident maybe they would never have gone further. Maybe they would not have come with a knife one year later. Maybe, with sex education well adapted for kids they would not have done what they did to me either. Maybe if I read about "rape" and "crime" instead of "forced sex" and "forced love" I would have gone immediately to the police because I would have been able to name what happened. Maybe I would not have had to go the police at all because when I was first harassed, bystanders would have helped me and prevented him raping me.

Maybe because I and everyone would have known that my body is mine, my consent is mandatory and no-one, absolutely no-one is entitled to me, it would never even have happened.

- Instagram https://www.instagram.com/alysealive/
- http://www.mastergenerecomunicacio.org/es/observatori

o/mujeres-valientes-por-una-nueva-informacion-sobre-las-violencias-sexuales/

- https://m.informarsobreviolenciamachista.com/
- http://aadas.org.es/

I DID IT FOR HER

BY SASHA MIDOU

Over twenty years ago, on my sixteenth birthday, one of my teachers showered me with gifts, cards and poetry. He had been my teacher since I was twelve and had been asked to leave the school quietly after an affair with another student. We were still in touch as he offered extra classes out of school and I signed up. Charismatic, charming and eleven years my senior, I was sucked into what I thought was a love affair that the rest of the world just didn't understand. He said that he had never met anyone like me, that he couldn't live without me and that he was so in love that he couldn't control himself around me. What followed was four and a half years of rape and sexual abuse. I had never had sex before. He told me that the increasingly extreme and painful experiences he subjected me to were part of a normal adult relationship, and whenever I said no, he would accuse me of not loving him as much as he loved me. I became distanced from my friends and family as he controlled and monitored my every move and every day. There were moments of public groping and humiliation, acts of possessiveness and control that felt more shameful than the physical abuse. I tried to get away by travelling around the world and then going to a university in another city. He would always draw me back in. Finally, after being coerced into having sex with him once again, my "no's" getting quieter and quieter as he continued anyway, I became pregnant and knew enough was enough. After having an abortion, I fled to another city and told him over the phone it was over.

It was over several years of having normal, healthy sexual experiences with other people that it slowly dawned on me how extreme that experience was. My behaviour with other men was somewhat warped but as I was treated with respect, I gradually realised that what he had done was not part of "a normal adult relationship". I bounced from one abusive relationship to another, having no sense of how to keep myself safe or what love really was. In the end I hit rock bottom and knew I needed some help. I had had some counselling on and off over the years since that time, and I had spoken about what had happened. The counsellors had helped me begin to identify the abuse for what it was and gave me words for what had happened: "Grooming... abuse... mental and emotional manipulation... rape". I embarked on three years of working intensely on myself, eager to change the patterns of abuse that had become so engrained and normal for me. I read and read, joined support groups, went to counselling and began to heal and get my old, beautiful sparkle back.

It was then that my counsellor offered to help me if I wanted to report what had happened. At the time there had been a new focus on rape and sexual abuse—particularly by men in positions of power and influence—and the media had started a new dialogue that felt like finally people like me might really be believed. As I heard the stories of the victims brave enough to waive their anonymity, to share their stories, and the encouragement for more of us to step forward, I began to consider reporting what had happened. Two other people had already contacted the police—one a teacher, another a barrister—who had known about him having multiple relationships with his students and had expressed concern that he was still working as a teacher. The police contacted me at the time, but I was too weak and broken to meet with them.

When I felt strong enough, I contacted Rape Crisis to find out how they could support me in reporting what had happened to me to the police. Initially I spoke with someone over the phone who was very sensitive, kind and respectful. I was shaking and emotional and alone. She treated me as if I was a hero just for dialling the number. The focus was on my courage for making the call and on making sure I was okay with every step of the conversation. She stopped me from going into too much detail, knowing I would have to repeat it all in person later. I made an appointment to visit the centre and headed there by myself. Some friends and family members know what happened to me, but my family in particular always found it hard to grasp the reality and severity of it, and in a way so did I. I think they needed me to be strong and okay, and so it was minimised, pushed aside and treated as something I should have gotten over by now.

When I arrived at the centre I was shown into a warm orange room with sofas and tissues. The woman I spoke to was one of the most sensitive, eloquent and protective people I've met. Everyone I interacted with at Rape Crisis seemed to have been put through some kind of Super Ninja Angel training where they had such reverence for the survivor, such tact and kindness that it was hard to hold it all together. It had been a long time since I had been at the receiving end of such kindness. I told my story, although because it was four and a half years' worth of incidents, she encouraged me to only go into as much detail as I felt I wanted to, knowing I would have to repeat it to the police. At the end she asked what I would like to do, and I said I was ready to report to the police. She explained my options and another meeting was arranged where I would arrive half an hour early to meet with her and ground myself a bit before the police officer would arrive. She asked me if I had any other questions and I asked her how much this was all going to cost me. She looked confused. "It won't cost you anything," she explained. "If the CPS decide there is a case then it is in their interest to prosecute him". I burst into tears. Up until that point I had thought that I'd need to use all my savings to do this.

So once again I returned to the centre and the same woman met with me. We talked through the plan and she explained that she would be in the room with me the whole time, but that she would not be able to speak or contribute to the police interview. The police woman arrived. She was a lot less sympathetic and looked quite weary and cynical. I tried as best I could to document every incident I could remember over those four and a half years. She wrote it down and asked some questions to clarify some things. I mentioned the other student he had had an affair with, but she interrupted me to say that that was just "hearsay" and that I should stick to what he had done to me. I also mentioned the other people who had contacted the police to express concern about him. I got a similar response. By the end of the conversation I felt exhausted and somewhat misunderstood and a bit silly and small. I tried to remember that everything I said was true and that this was the hardest thing I'd ever done (apart from survive those awful years). She explained that I needed to be willing to see the case through if we were going to take it further, that it wasn't just a matter of making a statement and then assuming my part was done. That the next step would be a video interview where I would need to go into as much detail as possible about what happened and then possibly further questioning. The man in question would then be contacted to be told what I was accusing him of and who I was and then he would be questioned. After that a decision would be made as to whether the case would go any further. I should be ready and willing to go to court and see it through to the end. I was pretty overwhelmed and didn't really know what I was actually capable of seeing through, but I nodded in agreement. After she left I spent some time with the woman from Rape Crisis and then I headed home in the rain.

I felt like I was going to faint. I wanted my mum. I wanted a hug, but I settled for a cup of hot, sweet, strong tea from a café on the way back to the station. Coming alone was a mistake and I promised myself to make sure someone came with me next time. Some friends called to see if I was okay. But I couldn't talk any more. I was completely spent. I went home, changed out of my wet clothes and lay on the floor in a foetal position for the twenty minutes I had left before I had to go back to work. Then I dragged myself back up and headed back out.

The woman from Rape Crisis met me at a café near the police station and we spoke briefly in preparation for my video interview. I had spent the last few days going through old diaries and emails, trying to remember every incident and to find any evidence that might help me. What I found were the beautiful, naïve words of an innocent young woman who was desperate to be loved, who was trying to make sense of this confusing and painful time, who was full of sparkle and hope. It broke my heart. I wanted to gather her up in my arms and tell her just how awesome she was. How precious she was. I decided then that whatever happened I would do this for her. For that beautiful young Me whose story needed to be told. Who deserved to be seen and heard and healed.

It was my first time in a police station and it was pretty dismal. I was introduced to the same police officer who had taken my statement and another, friendlier looking police officer. The first would be in the room with me asking the questions and the second would be watching the video to check that everything had been covered. My Rape Crisis advocacy rep would sit in another room and wait. I was led to an airless room with no windows and strip lighting in the basement of the station. The cameras in the wall were pointed out to me and the officer explained how things would proceed. And then the recording had started, and I was telling my story, trying to remember every detail and incident that happened over those four and a half years, over twenty years ago. She asked me how he'd have known that I wasn't consenting. I replied that sometimes I said no, sometimes I pleaded with him, sometimes I cried and other times I didn't, I just hoped that if I sounded like I was enjoying myself it would end a bit faster. When she asked me a third time I started to get upset. "I didn't fight him off if that's what you're asking me". She said that she was just trying to clarify the details. I described other incidents where I was coerced into doing something I didn't want to do. She then would repeat the story back to me, trivialising it and changing my words. I tried to reiterate and correct it, but there were other times where I just nodded.

I was in that room for almost two hours. It was one of the hardest things I've ever done. At the end I felt exhausted, misunderstood, misinterpreted, BUT: I did it. I told my story. It was on tape. It was out there. It was official. Not just some dirty secret in my head, or some unofficial, vague event that I'd half-told some of my friends, but a real thing. A crime that had been properly reported. I left the room and was shown back out of the building. Two of my friends were in the waiting room. They weren't even sure if I was there or not as no-one would confirm if I was in the building for security reasons. I fell into their arms and cried and cried. They led me back to the station and took me home. Another friend arrived with food and I sat, dumb struck and exhausted as they pottered around me, looking after me, feeding me and comforting me. I had cancelled the rest of my work and just stayed at home, drifting in and out of sleep.

I had to meet with the police a couple more times after that. Once to hand over evidence—my precious diaries from all those years ago, full of cringey teenage poetry and confused justifications—and another to help them make sense of the diaries. My dad came with me that time. I could see from the way he looked at me that it had finally dawned on him what I'd been through and what it took to go through this process. Being in a real-life police station and talking with real-life detectives is a pretty sobering experience. No longer could we pretend that it was just a half-real thing that was just too awful to really acknowledge. He witnessed how much it took out of me and how exhausted I was afterwards, and I finally began to be seen. Really seen. And understood.

I had a newfound respect for this young woman who was brave enough to walk to and from police stations and look detectives in the eye and tell her story, negotiating the law and the system with her head held high.

It took its toll. Knowing he was being interviewed. Knowing he knew I'd spoken up. Wondering if he'd track me down, find a way to communicate with me. I became worried about my presence online—my social media pages—full of pictures and opinions and comments that all could now possibly be used against me. I started to scrutinize every word and outfit and felt shame at the strangest things. I even worried I looked too happy or was dressed too confidently for someone who was really a rape victim. What should I wear and how should I present myself to prove it had really happened?

The case dragged on and the contact at Rape Crisis would periodically get in touch—both with me and the police. I was often relieved to hear there was still no news. I wasn't sure what I was hoping for—a decision that there was enough of a case to take this to court? Another few years of this hanging over my head, being cross-examined, having every word that young me wrote scrutinized and picked apart, being in the same room as him…. Or the crushing blow that actually there wasn't a case here, that it would not be taken further?

My contact at Rape Crisis changed jobs and a handover meeting was arranged. I met my new contact. She was also respectful and kind but not quite as switched on and dynamic as the first. I didn't feel quite as safe. She often sent text messages with words like "police" in them. They would pop up on my phone while I was at work and I'd hurriedly hide them. I asked a couple of times for her to be careful with her wording in text messages. She apologized and agreed, but after a while she went back to talking quite freely about the case in her messages. I didn't quite have it in me to argue any more.

After a year I finally got the call I'd been dreading. I took a moment to gather my thoughts and prepare. I decided that whatever the outcome, I would accept it and move forward accordingly. That I had done all I possibly could and the rest of it was out of my hands. Luckily it was the nicer officer who spoke with me and gently explained that the decision had been made not to take the case any further. She then explained all the approaches they had taken. They first looked at whether there was a case of grooming to be made. The problem was that the law that recognized grooming as a crime was passed in 2003. My case had happened before that. So then they looked at him being in a position of power and influence over me. Ironically, because he had already been asked to leave the school because of his affair with the other student, he wasn't officially my teacher anymore, and so they couldn't prosecute him for that. They then looked at each individual incident that I had reported, but most of them happened in a room with no other witnesses a long time ago and with no forensic evidence. And my diaries. For every page that described something unwanted or confusing there were ten that described how in love I was. The detective said that she didn't feel it was right to have the defence cross examine me and use my own words against me if there wasn't a really good chance we could win. And for that it needed to be proved "beyond reasonable doubt". There just wasn't enough evidence.

I listened quietly to everything she was saying, trying to take it all in and accept it. I felt devastated and also relieved.

She said she believed me. She said she knew what kind of a man he was and that she was very concerned about him continuing to work with children. She said she would be meeting with social services and the school to discuss the case and her concerns but then it would be in their hands how they monitored him or what, if any, action was taken.

She said the system was so flawed. That she saw it all the time and witnessed so many people get away with it, so many people cross examined in such harsh ways and so much misunderstanding around the word "consent" etc....

I tried to gather my thoughts and remember any questions I had. Had they contacted any of the teachers who knew he was in a relationship with me? She said it had been so long ago that most of the teachers had left and no records were kept that far back. Had she interviewed the two people who had contacted the police about him? She didn't even know about them and hurriedly took down their names.

I was pretty raw after that call. I knew I wouldn't appeal the decision because although it hadn't been as thorough an investigation as I'd hoped, I knew there just wasn't enough evidence to make a difference to the outcome. When I spoke with the woman at Rape Crisis she said the system was broken. It made me think about all these people working within a system that they know is so flawed, trying anyway to get a win, make a difference any way they can.

It's pretty bizarre to come face to face with the reality of the justice system. It suddenly wasn't something obscure and intangible that affected other people's lives, but something very real and, yes, flawed at best.

I had to think hard about my concept of justice. I had to think about what I believed in, did I have enough faith to trust in karma? In some kind of divine justice? I had managed not to think about him much and tried to actively keep focusing my energy and attention on me. This had always been about doing right by me. But I knew that no one capable of those horrific acts could be happy.

I had spoken up in order to pass the pain and weight of what had happened over to the right authorities, so I didn't have to carry it any more. And back to him too. He could live with it now.

I went through a grieving. For two weeks I was exhausted and was in bed by 9pm. Then I was angry at everyone and everything. And then I was just numb. I carried on working. It didn't occur to me not to.

I asked for some counselling and Rape Crisis said they offered some free sessions but there was a six-month waiting list. I looked into private counselling but haven't quite found the right person.

A friend took me out shopping and we bought bright flowy sexy dresses that I would never have chosen for myself. At first I pulled at them, trying to stop them from clinging to my body, but when she took a photo of me I saw a beautiful woman in a flattering outfit.

Another friend took me dancing and I tentatively experimented with dancing with men.

All my friends are getting married and having children. I long for that and hope that this will somehow help me move forward with all I wish for in my life. For now, I'm getting used to my new look and feeling safe around men again.

I met once more with the officers and my advocacy rep to collect my diaries. I was a bit of a state when I arrived, but we ended up not only talking about my case but the justice system in general. I could tell we were all on the same side. I could see that they were as frustrated as me and I felt heard and understood and respected and believed.

It's not fair. It's not fair. It's not fair. But I could go crazy with the injustice of it or I can face forward now, knowing I did all I could with the odds and the system stacked against me. I did right by that beautiful, young woman and I'm glad I spoke up.

PERFECT RAPE, IMPERFECT JUSTICE
BY PHOEBE

I never actually made a choice to report the first full-blown rape at the age of twenty-one. It was way out of my hands like *everything* else about the experience and much like a lot of my life before that. Looking back now, after years of therapy, I can see who I was. I was a vulnerable young (god, so young) woman, with a lot of bravado but deeply scarred already.

I'd had a difficult childhood, controlled, abused and too much responsibility for young shoulders to bear. So I was a bit of a mess already. I drank a lot, I screwed around, I had been assaulted a few times in clubs and I'd been used (but usually on the right side of consensual).

I went out and got drunk with some friends as many students do. I was walking home in the early hours but only separated from my friends for the last few hundred yards. Someone started speaking to me. I'll admit to start with I wondered if he'd be attractive—classy right?

As he approached I realised I didn't fancy him, but he kept asking me to "go somewhere". I was so close to home, but I was so far from safe. I think I went through every possible response. I tried befriending—I told him if he was less pushy he could probably find a nice girl. I tried to give him advice on picking up women. I got angry and screamed and swore at him. I fought, I bit him till he bled, and he barely flinched. Finally, I broke. And the war was lost.

Two girls in pyjamas came out of the flats. My angels in pyjamas. I remember thinking that surely in all those flats there would be at least one big burly bloke who would have responded to my screams but the girls that came to my rescue, they were so young and in their pyjamas. I thought it odd. I thought it sad that only they had come out.

They obviously called the police, so I didn't get that choice. They say you shouldn't make someone talk about something traumatic immediately after it's happened—but that's exactly what they do, the police—I know they need to, but it should be acknowledged that what they do—taking that statement is according to health advice, potentially harmful in and of itself.

I was used to feeling powerless growing up but just never with strangers, my bravado meant I never actually *felt* powerless even when being used by men who had no interest in me as a human being. But now, it was like a lifetime of powerlessness suddenly crashed through my façade of invincibility.

But it didn't stop when he stopped. The police took me home to get a change of clothes. They took me to a room with a sofa and a phone and a giant flower on the wall. I was still in my soiled clothing and I had been made to speak about every unspeakable thing that had just happened. I asked if I could bring someone and they told me "it would be easier if I didn't". For who would it be easier?

They let me make a phone call. One of my friends came to the station but no one would let her in. I have no idea how long I spent on that couch, but it was hours. Dirty, crying, bruised, alone—so very alone. I didn't own a mobile phone yet. Eventually they said they'd found a doctor, so I was taken somewhere else a good twenty minutes away I think.

And then? Well it was like the attack was just carrying on. I was told to strip in room full of officers, chatting and laughing about their own lives and concerns. The male doctor looked at all the parts of me, I never wanted anyone to look at, least of all now, when I felt like... well... like *this*. They wrote notes and called out injuries, took photos. It's like I wasn't even there. Except it was like I was also there *too much*.

I felt so disgusting that by the time I could have a shower, it was like the water wasn't touching me. I was an object first for him and then for them. It doesn't feel enough to say I felt powerless, it's just... it's just not *enough*. I felt like a broken puppet. The very concept of "power" or "control" was one I couldn't comprehend.

In many ways I was lucky, the police had their eye on someone, known to have tried it on several times in the area. They brought round photos and although it felt like I didn't know who it was, something inside me moved when I saw his face and again at the line-up. That's the only way I can describe it. Something moved my arm and my mouth said, "that's him". But it felt like my brain had no idea. Luckily for me there was a DNA match, as well as a "glitter" match (thanks to 90s fashion) to reassure me, but I couldn't quite make the connection feel real.

The way I was treated hardly helped me. I turned up alone to the line-up but the waiting room was full of others he'd tried it on with. Well others *and their boyfriends*. I couldn't find a seat. *Men were sitting down* next to their girlfriends and I was alone, and I couldn't sit down. I think that is the most alone I have ever felt in my life. It makes me angry now, and it felt so important and it broke me a little bit more. It made me even less worthy. Even less human. Even less like a real person.

Then came all the court prep. The defence were horrible, and I still don't understand why I was put in a room with them. The lawyer commented that I had quite large breasts, and asked how low my top was that night. I was petrified of court. I was given a little tour and the process explained, but I was still terrified. There were no advocates in those days. It was the police who kept dropping round to my flat to speak to me about updates in the case. At the very last minute he pled guilty. I felt I *should* have been relieved but a part of me had become a bit more ready to tell my story and it felt like now even this was taken off me.

That's not to say I wasn't lucky—he was caught, and he pled guilty and he was convicted. That's not the usual story and I am glad that it was successful in that way. I just never had a voice. The "last" step was the sentencing. I don't know why I went. To hear mitigating factors, almost all of which could equally have applied to me. To listen to his sob story and then to watch him grin at me from barely a few feet away from me. I felt sick. And I felt raped by the courts. Where was my voice? Why did no one speak for me? Why didn't anyone want to hear how much it *hurt*?

He was convicted for sexual assault. I was *raped*. He was out in 2 years. Here I am in 2017 still thinking about this, writing about this, feeling trapped and broken by this. I coped again by drinking and screwing around, but now I was even more vulnerable and I had to have even more bravado that sucked up all my energy. I locked parts of myself away and I fought hard to survive. Enduring flashbacks when with an entitled and abusive stranger you've picked up in a club leads to more rape. That embodied experience of the *absolute limits of your ability to be heard or to fight back*. That *embodied knowledge* that there are men who just don't care. That embodied experience of *absolute vulnerability* and fear leads to disempowerment, a small scared life, a world that terrifies you and often to more dangerous situations where you feel unable to do anything but carry out whatever is asked of you.

Rape is an abuse of power, it treats you as an object, a receptacle, a tool. You are ripped of any humanity and used for someone else's purpose and that's exactly how I felt treated during the entire process of reporting, despite my successful outcome. Alone, not human and broken. To gain back any sense of even a grain of control felt beyond impossible. I think the experience of fighting him broke me almost more than anything else. I came face to face with the absolute limits of my ability to fight back. I tried my *very hardest* and I couldn't stop it.

After the process I'd been through with the police even when I had been attacked by the "perfect rapist", an illegal immigrant, who pounces on unsuspecting women on the street—I felt unable to contemplate reporting rape to the police again for a very, very long time. How could I, when even this experience had resulted in questions about the clothes I had been wearing and comments about the size of my breasts?

REJECTION, POWER, AND RAPE
BY PHOEBE

I was twenty-one or twenty-two, picking up some thirty-something guy in a nightclub only a year or so after having been raped by a stranger in the street (2000). It may seem like a strange thing to do, but it was my way of coping with everything—to show the world I couldn't be broken I guess—to keep going out partying and bringing home men.

He was a regular and I used to work there. We were on our way home and things got heated in the car park and I started giving him a blow-job. Something about this triggers me, even though I am having a pleasant enough time. I don't know what it was, but in an instant I was transported back to that rape a year ago. I suddenly feel terrified—I am screaming, crying and shaking.

The guy is freaked out. Of course he is. I apologise over and over once I have started recovering—I had been walking home during the flashback and he's followed me. I obviously was not in the mood anymore and I think that most people would understand that, if not show some concern or even care. I just kept repeating "It's not your fault, it's not your fault" over and over and "I can't do this anymore" "I'm sorry, I can't do this anymore".

As I started to calm down I say to the guy, "I'm sorry, I was raped a while ago". Yeah, I apologised for having been raped. I could not have been less threatening, less insulting to his ego, or more vulnerable. "It wasn't anything you did—something just happened—I'm sorry, but I can't do this".

You know what, I was fairly cynical. I didn't expect this random guy to actually feel anything for me. I didn't expect him to be sympathetic or to care about the fact I had just had a flashback or that someone had raped me. I didn't expect him to walk me home, or hug me or show concern. I expected him to be a bit pissed off. That's probably why I apologised for having been raped, right? I expected him to whinge and walk away, annoyed he didn't get laid.

God, I wish he had, but he saw this wreck of a young woman, shivering, broken, vulnerable, apologising and telling him she had been a victim of crime and he said, "well you can't just leave me like this. You started this, you are finishing it". Stone. Cold.

No amount of saying sorry and no amount of being broken had triggered even a twinge of compassion in this man. My heart sank. Well, more like it burrowed its way down, down as far as it could. He looked determined. I kept apologising and saying I needed to go and I couldn't do this anymore. And he just coldly, consistently followed me, grabbing on to me, frog-marching me. I thought maybe he'd give up when he saw I wasn't changing my mind or he might get bored, or something. I tried a few times to get away from him, but I was already pretty broken I tried pleading—someone else had already done half his job for him. I was a mess. I thought maybe I could slip into the flat and shut him out. I kept being told "I had started it". I kept telling him he couldn't make me—or pleading that he wouldn't make me. What are you meant to do? Scream? Maybe. I couldn't. I was still recovering from a rape I had just relived.

He pushed his way into the flat despite my continued begging and explaining and apologising and trying "You aren't actually going to make me?", "Please just leave me alone", "I can't do it now".

All the while that my brain was trying to recover from this past trauma, this man was inflicting himself on me. I was crying the whole time. The memories are a blur, but they are painful, disgusting and humiliating. As he finished and got up and left, I managed to whisper, "you are a fucking wanker". He looked like he was going to hurt me again, but he just left.

The next time I saw him I ignored him. It's possible I even deigned to pull a face and told him he was a wanker. He became violent, screaming and shouting that I was a "lying bitch". I managed to escape him and sat locked in the toilet listening to an endless string of expletives, abuse, insults and threats of violence from him until he was thrown out of the club.

Suddenly I realised why he'd been so angry. Apparently, I had accused him of rape. I didn't think I had, I think he knew better than I did what he'd done.

Now the club is gone, I don't know his name and I don't have witnesses who saw anything except a girl grab a guy and take him home that night. I submitted an anonymous report in 2014 and in 2017 I went to the police. I was reporting three incidents that day and this was the only one they got a pen and paper out for. It seems my responses were deemed to be obvious enough even for a man to understand that I did not want to have sex with him. Sadly though, there is little in the way of a trail to follow to find this guy. So it is under investigation but who knows what will come of it. Perhaps if I had found the support and courage to report earlier, maybe even the night I was locked in the toilet—if someone had suggested speaking to the police, I would have had witnesses and a better chance at justice. Now though—I don't know what will come of this. But I feel that at least I have done all I can now, to bring intelligence to the police and maybe back someone else up if they too report something similar happening around that time and place.

MEN ARE HUMAN BEINGS TOO
BY PHOEBE

I didn't initially report two of the incidents that happened to me in 2003 and 2010. I didn't name them as rape for many years. They happened after a rape that I did report (2000), and after another rape (2001) that is still in the process of being investigated which I have written about separately.

The reason it took so long, was simply that I was going through a lot emotionally and with my health. There was so much trauma and other emotional baggage that these incidents were too much to deal with as well. My brain boxed them away and left them for another time. I didn't have any space or emotional strength to think about them until it was years later. And I had no sense that I deserved justice, or to be heard. They got put away with a lot of other painful stuff that I didn't know what to do with. And though they affected me greatly, at times, my main coping strategy was one of avoidance.

I have since had years of therapy, a lot which was compassion-focused therapy, that made me more aware of my own needs and helped me to develop a way to attend to them. I think eventually something grew in me. A confidence in my ability to tell the story. A feeling that I deserved to have my story heard. A need to do as much as I could physically do in response to what had happened. The activist voice for a woman's right to consent and withdraw consent was getting stronger and even some of the dialogue in the media was becoming more progressive. This gave me strength. Oddly, the final trigger was being groped in a public place in 2014 and being exposed to extremely progressive attitudes from the police when I contacted them about this.

I will make this clear though—I would not have done anything without access to an Independent Sexual Violence Advocate; a safe, kind person to speak to about my experiences and talk through whether it was worth reporting for me personally. I initially filed anonymous reports as I still doubted that much could be done, but wanted to have the incidents on record, in case others came forward, but as time went on I developed a need to be sure I had done "everything" I could.

I had worked in the sexual violence support sector, so I knew that there was little chance of justice for the situations I was describing but something in me needed to know I had done everything—so I decided to go to the police directly. I was supported by another ISVA through this process.

It was during the process that I realised that deep down I had built some hopes for justice. I just hadn't noticed them until they were crushed, painfully into nothing. The officers had good intentions, the setting was informal but nevertheless the questioning was soul-crushing.

The first of these incidents happened when I was twenty-four years old after I met a man (late forties/early fifties) from a bondage website. It was, I thought, a meeting of two human beings. We went out for food and talked about normal things people—life, TV, fun, books. I had been clear from before the meeting—I was not into violent, abusive or rape play, but instead enjoyed toys and respectful exploration of the senses and bondage. I was also clear I didn't want anything "BDSM-y" to happen until there had been explicit discussion about safe words etc.... And I told him it was because I had been raped before. Looking back, I realise now that I was just signalling my vulnerability and suitability as a victim to a predator. I thought I was talking to a normal empathic human being—which is how he had seemed to be.

After the first night out, we kissed goodbye at the tube, I'd had a nice time, and it felt okay until he pinched my nipples so hard they bled. I was unhappy with this and texted him later from my hotel that maybe we shouldn't meet again as I didn't want to be hurt like that at all and that anything we were to do like that would need discussion, which hadn't happened. He reassured me we would not do anything else non-vanilla without talking first and apologised. He had got carried away and wanted to show me he fancied me. Perhaps I shouldn't have taken him at his word, but I did—because I thought he was a decent human being. Because I did not believe all men were rapists-in-waiting.

So we did meet up the next day and went to his house to feed and walk the dog before going out. Was this a naïve thing to do? The police certainly questioned the fact I had gone back to his place having met him on a bondage site. I felt stupid when questioned. Like it was stupid to trust a man to act like a human being. When we came in from walking the dog, things changed. He called me into the bedroom to show me something and when I got in he shut the door and stood in front of it. He ordered to me to undress. His voice was threatening. He was between me and the door. I tried to laugh it off, but he ordered me again. So I did it.

The questions from the police came. Why did you do it? Why didn't you say "no"? Why didn't you initiate a conversation about safe words then?

It felt too late. Don't forget how much trouble I had gone to, to explain to this man how much I did not feel comfortable with anything happening without discussion. He had reassured me the night before he wouldn't do anything else without talking first. I was extremely young, alone in a strange part of the country I had never been to before. I was aware that he had broken every promise and reassurance he had given me. He had shut the door to the room and stood in front of it. He had deliberately ignored everything I had said previously. He knew I was already vulnerable. He knew what had happened the night before had been too much for me.

So I was not able to say "no"—this felt like a dangerous man. I tried to say, "please don't hurt me". I tried to say, "please don't do this" but I was slapped repeatedly in the face and called a whore, a slut, and more. I couldn't get my words out. He pushed me on the bed, he forced himself in me and my mouth and anally. I sobbed throughout the whole thing. I did not participate in what was happening to me.

Afterwards he held me on the bed while I sobbed. I don't know if he thought this was comforting, but I just felt imprisoned. As I had no idea where I was, or how much more violent he could get—my survival instinct suggested to me to carry on as we had planned. We went out that night and I went home as early as I felt safe to. I texted him that that was nothing like what I had been looking for, that I was sorry, but I had not enjoyed it. I know that may seem a strange reaction, but I just didn't want to provoke someone I saw as dangerous any more. He never responded to my text and I never heard from him again.

The questions came from the officers, how did he know you hadn't just changed your mind? How did he know you didn't want him to do this? How did he know where the line is drawn for what things you wanted him to do and what things you didn't want to do were? Couldn't he have thought this was all part of the bondage and domination that you both have an interest in? Why didn't you ask for a safe word? You say you tried to speak, but did you actually get your words out? If not, how could he know you weren't happy with what was happening? You didn't meet on a normal dating site? Perhaps he just thought you had changed your mind?

To my mind, the only world in which these questions haven't already been answered is a world in which men aren't human beings with feelings or understanding or empathy, and are presumed to be completely incapable of seeing vulnerability or have any ability to see that they are acting in a threatening way.

To my mind, the only question left unanswered is: given everything I had told him, what made him think that was what I wanted to happen at that moment, having not had a discussion about what we would or would not try or any discussion of safe words?

The second of the incidents for this part was a drunken one in 2010, with a friend. Yes, we had previously had drunken consensual sex on occasions (nothing serious) but not for a few years before this incident. I had at one point liked him a lot more than he liked me, but I'd got over that by then. I no longer fancied him and in fact I was beginning to see how unattractive some aspects of his personality were when it came to women. I was surprised he made any advances given all this.

We shared a cab to the train station from the pub but when we pulled up, I got scared of the long journey ahead to get home in the dark. He asked if I wanted to go back to his instead and he kissed me. I pulled back and said that I'd appreciate a bed, but that sex was definitely not on the cards. I asked him if that was okay and he agreed. We went back to his and I asked for a duvet for the couch. He brought me weed and more drink. We were both very drunk. I kept trying to refuse any more, but he was persistent, so I had a bit. I told him the weed would make me sleepy, but he kept on at me. I was getting sleepier and sleepier, but he wouldn't go to bed. He kept insisting there was nothing to sleep on the sofa with and to just share the bed and stop being silly. He threatened to chuck me out if I wasn't going to join him. He said there was no point me being there. I said I had no money, there weren't any trains. I had nowhere to go.

I said we could kiss and I would sleep in the bed if he was going to be like that—but we were not having sex. Not in a million years.

I needed sleep so badly, but I repeated many times that nothing was happening except kissing. He agreed, and I got into bed dressed. He pestered me a lot, trying to kiss me more, trying to take my clothes off. Saying there was no point me staying unless we had sex. I kept pushing him off and telling him to get off me and that I just wanted to sleep. Things get kinda blurry from here as I was extremely sleepy/passing out from the drink and the weed.

I kept saying no. I tried to move away. I tried to turn away. I tried to push him off me. I knew what he was saying, but he was an old friend. He knew about the things that had happened and I never believed he would cross that line.

At some point, though his face changed. He stopped holding back. He shoved himself on top of me and started forcefully removing my clothing. I told him to stop but he carried on. I couldn't now get him off me. He wasn't even trying to kiss me, he was just single-minded, and he was in me. At that point I cried, and I pleaded for a condom, but there was no stopping him now.

I don't remember much of what happened. I know he came. I know I felt sick. I know I tried to turn away. I know I wasn't reciprocating or actively participating. I know it was nothing like the other times we have had sex. I know that even though I packed it away in my head later, so I didn't rock the boat or cause a fuss or potentially be called a liar, I had also got rid of every photo I had of him that day. I know that even though when he pestered me to go out drinking and I agreed, I would also cry myself to sleep in the night.

He was my friend and I didn't want to believe what had happened. I wanted to think there was still good in him. I didn't want him to deal with the shame of what he did, so I didn't tell him. He acted like he couldn't remember what happened and I couldn't bring myself to explain otherwise. We went out drinking a couple of times though most of the time I tried to avoid him.

Eventually there came a time when he asked if he could stay in my spare room for a while. I suddenly realised just how much I didn't want him near me. I was also struggling, and he kept pestering to come and support me with my issues, to take me out for a drink and a chat. I was crumbling under the pressure of having to keep telling him no and him not listening to me. Eventually I realised I had to tell him why I never wanted to see him again. So I sent a text—I stopped carrying the memories by myself and let him take them—I asked that he never contact me again. He never replied to the text. Apparently, he showed it to my friend and claimed he didn't remember that night but agreed he shouldn't get in touch with me again.

The police questions were so similar again. Why didn't I get out of the bed and go sleep on the sofa? Why did I get into bed with him? Why didn't I leave? If I asked for a condom, was I saying yes to sex with a condom? How did he know I didn't want to have sex with him? How did he know I hadn't changed my mind? Women change their minds. Had I consented by agreeing to have sex in exchange for a bed for the night? Did I have sex out of obligation, even though I didn't want to?

I couldn't verbalise in the interview what had happened in a way that the officers understood. I hadn't had sex with anyone. I had not participated in this act. I had repeatedly said no and trusted a friend not to just get on and violate my body despite this. Yes, we had had sex before. But that was the difference— I had been a part of the act. This was something different. Any movements I made had been futile attempts to get him off me or turn my body away. Most of the time that I remember I was frozen. I was shocked he would continue doing this to me, despite no response from me. I wasn't consenting by not getting out of bed, I wasn't able to get out of bed. He knows what it is like to have sex with me consensually—this was not it. He knew I had nowhere else to go. He knew I always saw the good in him, even when he was being an idiot. He knew I had been raped before. He knew I would want a condom no matter what. Is asking for a condom consenting to sex? Isn't it just asking for some mercy—"don't shoot me, take my money"? Is asking for a condom, and him penetrating your body without one, consenting to sex?

Why was I only reporting now? Something to do with him having a girlfriend now? Was I jealous? And again—how did he know I didn't want to? And why did I stay—in the house—in the bed? Sometimes women say no and change their minds.

If I had changed my mind, I would have been a participant of what was happening. He would have known it if I had changed my mind. Even if I had done it despite not wanting to, he would have been a partner in an act, not a sole actor with me as an object. I have slept with over one hundred men. One-night stands. Many men are disrespectful. One man urinated in my bed after sex. One man whined and whined till I agreed to have sex with him. I cried in the toilets and then came out and I had sex with him. I have had rough consensual sex. I participated in that. As rough as it was, I was listened to when I said "enough". I have had sex tied up and I have tied up men. I have been choked and smacked and called names. Sometimes I have been pressured into it and sometimes not.

But I know when I am doing something I don't want to do because I am still doing it. I wasn't doing anything with these men—they were violating my body.

This process has only just been bearable because of support from my ISVA but I cannot blame the officers themselves entirely, though I feel their methods could be improved. They are asking the questions the defence and jury will want to know the answers to. They only put forward cases that would survive this questioning as that is what's needed for a conviction. Whatever the officers believe, the answers to these questions are what a jury will use to decide if someone is guilty, so I am glad my story has been tested without needing to go through that process in court.

But I feel angry that I feel interrogated and broken again, and the men have not had to answer a single question about their behaviour. They walk free, safe and invincible. It took me till 2017 to build up the courage to tell the police and it feels like that courage and hope for justice was trampled on that day at the station.

The lesson I learned from this process is that there is only one reason I would ever report to the police and that is if my need to report for its own sake became great enough to compel me to do it. Because there are no guarantees—that's an understatement. And more than that the process itself, even before prosecution or conviction is painful and soul-destroying and the system does not compensate us for that in any way. So for me, I would only do it, I felt I needed to—for myself and only if I had an advocate to support me.

Maybe some of you reading this still believe this is not rape or criminal. And maybe legally it isn't at this time. If that's the case I believe it should be. Because this is not sex. This is not a grey area.

I have had sex many, many times with many men and only a

tiny percentage of that in anything vaguely resembling a respectful relationship and yet these two incidents stand out to me as uniquely damaging, violent, and dehumanising. These two incidents out of hundreds of drunken one-night stands with men who wanted nothing more than a quick use of my body, stand out as events that deprived me of basic human rights and deeply traumatised me. They should be treated as crimes because I do not believe that most men, in this society would ever consider doing anything remotely like these acts, or would want to experience them themselves. And yet the questions we ask victims seem to hint that most men would do this to someone's body, unless they were explicitly, assertively and skilfully fought off or resisted.

This makes me feel broken and angry and betrayed by society. This makes me feel that the public largely believe that men cannot be trusted, and women are stupid to trust them. This makes me wonder how many thousands of these incidents occur and are never recorded even after attempts to report to the police (which is only a small percentage of those that happen). This makes me wonder if the public will ever understand what consent is and whether women will ever really be in control of their own bodies? There is no justice at this time for me. I cannot receive any form of compensation or hear remorse, or force any of these men to face up to the damage they have caused.

JUSTICE DISSUADED
BY KIRSTY

I went straight to the police. After I left the party with a friend, I saw a police car stationed on Sauchiehall Street. I marched right up to it.

"I'd like to report a sexual assault", I told the officer who rolled the window down. "Someone just tried to rape me".

They drove me and my friend straight to the police station, where I was asked to sit in a waiting room. I went into the bathroom and sat down in one of the cubicles. I had the worst panic attack of my life; I actually thought I was having a heart attack. When it passed—whether it was a minute or an hour I have no idea—I went back out into the corridor.

A female police officer was waiting for me there, and she led me into one of the interview rooms. She wrote down everything I could remember, asking very few questions and being very supportive. She commented that it was great that I wasn't too drunk. "It shouldn't matter, but people are more likely to believe you", she confided. They took my friend's statement in a different interview room.

After they had taken my statement, the officer told me what would happen next. Someone would be over in the morning to pick me up for a second statement—"in the light of day"—and they would see if they had enough to press charges from there.

When I got home it was already getting light. I tried to sleep, but didn't get any before the buzzer went. I buzzed them up, and threw on a jacket to go out. Two minutes later I was answering the door to two police officers, one male and one female. They wanted to know if the kitchen was okay to conduct the interview in.

Being a student living with three other students, my flat was slightly less than immaculate. It was probably tidier than most student accommodation, but I still remember feeling ashamed at the dirty dishes and empty bottles as I led them into the kitchen. If I had known they would come into my flat like this, I would have tidied up a little. I feel, in hindsight, that to enter someone's personal space without warning, especially after they've been through an event like I had, is wrong. I already felt like my privacy and control were violated. Now I had to describe this violation in detail to two strangers, in my flat. I had flatmates who I didn't want to find out about the attack. Police officers in our kitchen would raise a few eyebrows.

I poured three glasses of water, and sat down at the table with them.

The officers took a statement from me. They would ask me questions, usually yes or no questions, and I would give short answers. They would then write this down as a statement. For example, if the officer asked, "did he hold you down at this point?", and I responded, "yes", they would write down, *He tried to hold me down at this point*.

This statement is then evidence to potentially be used in court—as if you said it.

The statement went on for a while. I was still in shock, so my communication was less than perfect. The kept having to go back over details. I knew that the previous evening I had remembered everything, and had told the officer at the station everything. But now it was getting hazy. I remembered him getting on top of me. Then I remembered having a panic attack somewhere else in the building, and calling a friend to come and get me.

This is normal for survivors, and I know that now. But every time I seemed unsure of the details, the male officer would raise an eyebrow and let the silence drag out for a few seconds too long before asking me another question. I started to tell them what I'd told the other officer, the night before—but that was from my memory of that interview, not the actual event.

About halfway through my statement being taken, my flatmate walked in. She paused in the doorway, said hello, then got something from the fridge and left. I would have to make up a story for her.

They read my statement back to me, to make sure they had gotten everything correct. There were several errors. I had told the officers that the man had used a doorstop to wedge the door closed. The statement said that he had wedged the door *open*. The implications of each are completely different. They had written down in the statement that I was a lesbian. This is untrue, and highly irrelevant either way. I got them to remove this part of the statement, change the errors, and then signed the bottom of the last page.

The officers then spoke to me about the process. They described how the police would be dealing with my attacker. It was his party I'd been at, so all our mutual friends would know very soon, they warned. They described the stress my attacker would currently be going through. They wanted to know if I still considered him to be a friend. They had already arrested him based on my accusation the previous evening, and he had spent the previous night in jail. They would be taking statements from him right now.

"So, if you're not sure that this is what really happened", the male officer told me, "now's the time to say so". The female officer interjected a few times with more supportive comments, sometimes even contradicting her colleague. But mostly it was the male officer who spoke.

Then they told me that it was unlikely the case would even come to trial. There was no physical evidence, unfortunately. I'd managed to punch him in the face and get away. Unfortunately. It was my word against his. So I'd be going through a lot of stress and they would be going through a lot of paperwork, all for nothing.

My hand, holding my glass of water, had been shaking uncontrollably for quite a while as he said this. The male officer took a long look at it before saying,

"You're clearly already upset about it, and we haven't gotten to the difficult stages yet. Unless you're doing that on purpose?"

I tried to stop shaking but couldn't.

They described the stress of a trial in some detail. Having to give evidence in front of the man who tried to hurt you is difficult, the male officer told me. "But they can put up a screen, so you don't have to see him", the female officer quietly interjected. I would have to describe the "incident" in front of lots of people—but you can have an advocate to support you.

As they spoke, I stopped listening. They were drowned out by my own imaginings of the trial. I was studying linguistics and wanted to pursue a career in language policy. To this end, I had written an essay on the language used in court a few weeks earlier, focusing on vulnerable witnesses—including rape trials. I had read page upon page of transcripts of rape and sexual assault trials. Lawyers talking about women's menstrual cycles in detail. Lawyers holding up items of clothing—dresses, underwear—to be scrutinised by the jury. "If that's a dress—if we can call that a dress". Women's sex lives being analysed and dissected.

I told them I would drop the charges.

I was so torn. I wanted to get this man behind bars, and I

wanted to stand up for myself and for other survivors. I'd been raped before, years previously, and hadn't reported it. My attacker had gone on to rape a friend of mine, and had then beaten her within an inch of her life when she threatened to go to the police. That was on my head. I wanted to do the right thing this time—not for me, but for other potential victims.

But all the transcripts I'd read and stories I'd heard stopped me. These officers, painting a vivid picture of how difficult the trial process would be, stopped me. I couldn't do it. I just wasn't strong enough. So I would drop the charges.

Then they explained the way sexual assault charges work in Scotland. It's not the victim who presses charges, but the Crown Office. And I'd just made a statement saying it happened to the Crown Office. If I didn't want to go ahead with the trial, I'd have to retract my statement. Say that I was mistaken.

In my statement, I'd told them that I'd been raped in the past, and had gotten a little emotional about it at the party. I had my first appointment at the Rape Crisis Centre later that week, and so it had been on my mind. Perhaps, the male officer suggested, I was upset about the previous attack, and what was intended as a hug had been misconstrued by myself. An understandable mistake.

I agreed to change my statement so that it read that.

The officer told me it was okay that I'd been mistaken, and it was good that I'd come forward right away and admitted it, for everyone involved.

"No", I corrected him. "I wasn't mistaken. I know he tried to rape me. I know that if my instincts hadn't kicked in, if I hadn't punched him in the face, I would have been raped last night. I'm only saying that for the statement, so I don't have to go through the trial process".

Neither of the officers had a problem with that. They packed up and left.

They say that hindsight is twenty-twenty. Looking back, the treatment by the police officers makes me angry. They intruded upon my personal space, insinuated that I was lying or mistaken, cared more about irrelevant facts like my sexuality than the truth, and made me feel ashamed for what had been done to me. Now, several years later, I've been through one-on-one counselling at university and at Rape Crisis. I've also been to group counselling at Rape Crisis. Mostly for the previous rape, although this attack did come up a few times. I have come to terms with what happened.

I'm also proud of the way I acted. I managed to fight back, unlike the previous time. I also went to the police. As a result of that, this man spent the night in jail. Hopefully that's enough to deter him from attacking again. The only reason I didn't pursue it any further was a direct result of the officers who came into my home. That a potential rapist got off scot-free is on their heads, not mine.

The officers the night before, both those who drove me to the station and the officer at the station, were supportive. They gave me the time and space I needed to report what had happened, in as much detail as I could. They allowed me space to panic, and time to calm down, and offered support. They listened, instead of bombarding me with questions. They believed me, instead of raising eyebrows and sharing glances.

It was the officers the following day who allowed their personal feelings and weaknesses to cloud their objectivity. The male officer was certain I was lying, or couldn't be bothered with the paperwork. The female officer allowed him to act this way.

I know that, today, I would be strong enough to press charges. But I wasn't then—and that's okay. What's not okay is for it to be so difficult for a vulnerable person to press charges. After an attack, you don't feel strong or confident. I felt weak and ashamed. It took very little to persuade me to drop the charges, to lie and say I was "mistaken" about the events.

Before this happened, I had already been looking into careers in language policy. This event made me feel so much more strongly about that. The way statements are taken needs to be brought into the twenty-first century. Recorded interviews are much more reliable than the way I was interviewed. Even my statement; that of a native English speaker, was incorrectly transcribed. More vulnerable witnesses than me are interviewed every day. Recorded interviews allow less bias from police officers, and less room for misunderstanding. Unfortunately, the event is also the reason I couldn't follow that career—those police officers not only dissuaded me from bringing my perpetrator to justice, but also from following a career I felt passionate about and which I felt could make a real difference.

But what really needs to change is people's attitudes. The default stance towards survivors should not be that they are lying. Better training should be provided, and officers like those I encountered should not be allowed to deal with victims. We need to create a space for discourse about sexual assault—to confront the proverbial elephant in the room.

THEY BELIEVED ME
BY LEIGH

This is for those still standing, those still struggling, those no longer here and those yet to have faced the pain. I've learnt that silence kills, and solidarity is the only way forward when for women one in four of us will be forced to face and cope with the impact that rape and sexual assault have on us for the rest of our lives. I promise it will get better and you will move forward.

It was April 2011 in the UK, I was twenty years old. My relationship at the time was deteriorating, and I had little to no self-esteem. I'd started a new job and made new 'friends'.

The day prior to when the incident took place I remember I was walking through my town centre and subconsciously thinking how 'safe' I felt and how I hadn't felt like that before—maybe this thought made me ignorant or arrogant? What I do now know is I didn't ask for what happened, nor was it my fault.

On the evening of the incident I went out with those said 'friends', I drank alcohol before we headed to the location we planned to 'celebrate' at. In truth I didn't even want to be out with these new 'friends', but I felt I should as they were part of the same team at the new job I'd recently started.

Upon arriving at the venue, I met three males who we then spent the majority of the night with. They were friendly, and I believe the one I spent most of the time in conversation with had a girlfriend.

I accepted drinks from them and from what I can remember was enjoying myself—low self-esteem plus the attention they were giving, resulted in me feeling flattered. We danced and chatted, and they purchased drinks throughout the night.

The discussion at some point must have turned to their occupations—they were all soldiers serving in the British Army, just as my boyfriend was and this naively made me feel instantly 'safe'. There were two of us, my friend was male. According to the statements of those men and my 'friend' we agreed to go back to their hotel room.

I don't remember much, just snippets which aren't clear at all. I now know timeframe-wise we got to the hotel between 3–4am. I can't account for the next couple of hours, I believe I passed out and at around 6am I awoke to the perpetrator on top and inside of me.

My memory of the entire night is not completely clear, something I have questioned over and over again. There has been more than one occasion that I have doubted myself entirely, not knowing the entire truth and having to live with that lack of memory is something I'm still affected by to this day over six years on. However, something I specifically remember very clearly is being outside of the venue at closing time with the 3 males and attempting to leave only to be followed out of the outdoor area we were gathered in and being picked up by the perpetrator and taken back, whilst asking to be 'put down'.

When I awoke it took a few moments for me to realize what was happening. My arms seemed to be pinned down by either side of my body and I wasn't sure I could even move my legs. Almost as if my body was frozen still. I do remember starting to be aware that something awful was happening and been bitten on my shoulder blade—I remember saying no. Saying stop it and again no.

I also remember the perpetrator's acquaintance standing in the door way telling him to stop, too; 'just leave it'. While my 'friend' (apparently) lay none the wiser in the bed next to us.

I remember him getting off me and me rolling onto my side whilst I 'gathered' myself mentally before I got up and ran to the bathroom. I came out of the bathroom to my 'friend' who said we needed to leave and so I started to collect my belongings but couldn't find my knickers or tights. We found them—in the perpetrators hold-all.

When we left I knew something awful had happened, but I felt like a child again, knowing what had happened was wrong but not knowing or being able to articulate into words what it was.

The acquaintance I was with, to give him his due, was relatively sensitive to the situation and calmly told me that I'd been raped, and we should go to the police.

We did—I walked into the station and I said I had been raped. There have been moments over the years I have doubted that decision and wished I'd kept the revolting truth of that night to myself, but I don't for a minute now doubt I made completely the correct decision.

I was escorted to a room to wait for specialist officers to arrive. When they did it was a female and male officer. I instantly told them I didn't want the male in the room and he respectively and understandingly left the room.

I was asked what had happened and I explained. I had to use the bathroom to provide a urine and faeces sample to the lady officer. I was advised I could not have an examination at the station and would need to go to a special unit for this. The lady officer asked if there was anyone I could call, and I called my Mom—I don't remember exactly what was said or if I even said anything, but I know I found it difficult and so the lady officer took the phone and explained the situation to my Mom.

I went in a car to the special unit, with two female officers and my Mom and Step-Dad met us there. I had to have a full body examination—which aside from the rape obviously, haunts me to this day. Not that the doctor was anything but professional, he and the lady officer acting as chaperone kindly explained in full what would happen and why it needed to happen, which meant I fully understood and was prepared.

I lay on the examination bed and the tiles next to it were purple and green—I remember singing Barney (the dinosaur) song in my head whilst the doctor did an internal examination down below, what I can only describe as horrific. Not only had this man ripped me of my spirit, his horrendous violating act had resulted in another stranger, having to violate the most private part of my body all over again, yet I understood the whys and subsequent reasoning of this action.

I hope those reading can appreciate that with any trauma it's difficult to have a clear memory of events when those 'events' are not something you wish to think about—ever. I know already I will be one of few that feels they had a positive experience with the police.

At every opportunity they made me feel comfortable and as at ease as I could have felt. They never spoke to me in a condescending or patronizing manner. I believe I was lucky with the treatment I received, I shouldn't feel lucky, as it really should be the norm, but the attitudes of those I encounter within authority should not only be mandatory, training in how to deal with, the ever-growing victim rate, should be completed before any of those even speak with a victim.

I fall into the 15% that choose to report. My mother was the victim of domestic abuse and at a relatively young age I learnt she had been raped by my father—I do believe that this is why I knew I had to report; she never did. And I would not change that decision.

Although there was no 'lawful' justice reached which I must make clear, that same male officer from the very first encounter with those in charge of investigating took over speaking directly with me, he kept me informed of the process and treated me with the dignity I had deserved that night.

The three men involved had almost three weeks to ensure their 'stories' matched, I gave my formal statement the day following my reporting. The acquaintance I was with gave his statement the day I reported. The police informed me that he had admitted to giving each of the men oral sex in the hope 'they didn't do anything to me'. And that the three men had left the hotel room only ten minutes after we did. The police officer advised that the CPS would look at this as if it was a group of people having an 'orgy' and I had woken up regretting what 'I'd done'.

This couldn't have been further from the truth, but I understood the realistic advice the police were offering me to prepare me for the outcome from the CPS. The crown prosecution must look at how a defence barrister would pull apart 'my side of the story' and weigh up if considering the evidence this would result in prosecution.

Approximately—six to eight weeks after reporting the incident the officer called and asked if he could come to my home to discuss the decision the CPS had reached. He arrived and explained that the CPS would not be taking it any further due to lack of evidence.

Nothing had shown up from my toxicology tests and therefore it was my word against theirs.

The officer however wished to advise me in no uncertain terms that he and his team BELIEVED ME.

To this day I hold onto that statement. It's not justice, it's not anywhere near enough. But it was clarification to me that I was believed. And I will never let go of that. My statement will remain on record and if or when the perpetrator is to commit a further offence and it is reported there will be my statement awaiting use for this said purpose.

Police have to face some horrendous crimes, unimaginable: they should receive the best training that could be offered—from a survivor perhaps? And if they're not they should not deal with victims of crime of this nature—the effect the authorities can have on the recovery of a survivor of rape can be incredibly detrimental and I can't personally bear thinking about what would have been my recovery had I had a completely negative experience with the professionals we look to for support and for lack of a better word—justice.

If I can help just one person this traumatic crime is committed against find the strength and hope to report, then this is worth the anguish it has caused me writing 'my story'. Maybe one day when the true volume of victims come forward the authorities and society will be forced to accept the impact this crime has on so many and the offenders would be forced to take responsibility and face the punishment for their **crime**.

MEN ARE FROM MARS
BY VICTORIA

Have you ever that feeling when you wake up after the night before, you know that fuzzy foggy really can't remember and who the hell is that behind me kind of a feeling? That icky "god get them out of here and let no more be said about the matter" kind of feeling? Well I have, several times. One-night stands! I am a liberated woman what can I say? However, on the morning of the date in question I awoke with a similar feeling but this time it was more of a "who the eff is that going at me from behind" kind of a feeling.

I froze. I froze because for a second I couldn't think who I was, where I was, why this was happening—I was still drunk from the night before. I searched my mind looking for answers, but the copious amounts of alcohol consumed meant I simply could not remember. I had experienced a "black out". Or, as I was informed later by my investigating officer (IO) that, what I mean is, "I was just too pissed to remember".

Personally, I prefer the known and well used term "black out". Which does not mean "blacked out". Because blacked out means blacked out. My IO liked to keep reminding me of this, serving only to make me feel like a naughty schoolgirl.

I had a vague recollection of being awake at some point that morning; I remember looking out the window and seeing daylight. I remember thinking I was late for work. I looked at my phone, I didn't recall my alarm going off or anything. I was late. Memories from the night before came back to me slowly, as my brain chugged into gear.

I remember meeting my male friend from work late afternoon. We had met at work on a training course he delivered, he added me on Facebook and we struck up a friendship. We had met once before and something similar had happened. As in, he tried something on with me and I froze. I let it happen. I can't answer why I did this. I can't answer why I forgave it. I put it down it us both drinking and made it clear to him I never wanted this to happen again. In fact, I asked to make this a condition of the friendship were it to continue. He agreed. He said he understood. I trusted him.

I don't remember much that morning at all. I have vague memories of scrabbling around finding clothes for work, feeling sick when he referred to sexual activity the night before; of which I had no recollection. I barely remember my journey to work. I know I called my sister and she verifies this later, the details of the conversation unrecalled by me. She was clear what had happened and is a key witness in my case.

What I do remember is getting to work, closing myself in my office and staring blankly at my computer screen with tears streaming down my face. My boss called me and asked how my weekend was and what I had planned for the day. "I was raped last night" were the words that came out. I said it just matter of factly as I struggled to grasp the concept. I had to say the words out loud.

I know I was raped because I told him that day he came to visit. He must be one hundred per cent clear, I did not want to go "there" with him. I know I was raped because I had told him previously I black out easily when I drink, and he brought a litre bottle of JD "that night" and poured me drinks all night. I know I was raped because I remember him leaning in for a kiss the night in question and I pushed him away and said clearly "No". I know I was raped because I cannot recall anything further from that night, I was too drunk to have given consent. I do not know if I was spiked or if it was the alcohol that caused me not to remember. I know I was raped because, eight months on, I still feel a sickness to the pit of my stomach, a feeling of shame, humiliation and a disconnection between my body, myself and the world in which I live.

That man shattered my very being and orchestrated a situation in which he would get what he wanted from me.

Initially I spent a month or so going out and getting drunk, ignoring the gnawing in my stomach, ignoring the need to just sob and have someone hold me, tell me it was going to be ok.

I contacted the rape crisis centre, I couldn't seem to accept that I had been raped. This shouldn't happen to me, I am a strong independent woman. I felt foolish for having trusted someone. I feared the thought of police or the thought of his children and family being adversely affected by this if I reported it. They would suffer at the expense of his filthy lust. I felt foolish for having allowed someone in my house, to have drunk alcohol with them. I felt foolish for feeling such deep shame and deep depression—rape is something that happens by a stranger, with violence and down a dark alley in the seclusion and secrecy of nightfall. I felt guilty for calling this rape when my perception of rape previously was something so different. But the truth remains that consent could not have been given in my deeply inebriated state. These thoughts invaded my very existence and I could find no reprieve. I was haunted by feelings of disgust and shame.

The rape crisis centre staff were everything I would expect: empathic, kind, understanding. They said they would support me if I were to go to the police. How could I go to the police? When I invited this man into my home? I invited this to happen?

These were my thoughts and guilt shaped my existence.

I signed myself off from work with "stress". Work was stressful actually, but this, this was consuming me, I could barely walk out the house. I felt naked if I left the house, like everyone was staring and laughing at me. I couldn't eat unless it was bingeing on toast or cake. I could no longer go to the gym as I felt dirty and disgusting. I was marred, tainted, ruined.

One day, a month or so after it happened, I found myself walking up the steps to the police station, I don't even recall getting there. I turned and ran away before speaking to anyone but there was undeniably an urge within me to attempt to seek justice. And eventually I did.

I woke up one morning and just did it, it was like being on auto pilot, driven by the strong feeling that justice somehow must prevail. Sex without consent or without capacity consent is rape, no matter how you dress it.

The decision to report is not an easy one. Nor is the journey following. If I were to be honest, if I could turn back time I would not have reported. Simply because, for me, it hindered my recovery. Every meeting with the police, or advocate, or any other related tasks sent me into a vast and downward spiral into which I felt suicide was the only way out. Fortunately, I had referred myself to local mental health team who really helped me through this period. However, I self-harmed as a way to somehow release these feelings I was unable to express.

The police, initially were fantastic, they were sensitive and kept me informed. In less than a week I found myself taking part in the video interview—which is so difficult. As I could not recall a lot of the incident I guess it was easier than what some would face. Having to use words like "penis" and "vagina" to a stranger with a camera and microphones (although concealed you are very aware of their existence) felt like well, it was a form of humiliation I guess.

I was then promised, on a weekly basis, that he would be arrested that week. After a month of this I kind of lost hope and felt so disconnected and unsupported while trying to recognise of course there are lots of serious crimes they had to investigate and not just mine. But still, it hurts.

The day it happened I was at work. I got a call from the IO saying they were going to invite him in for voluntary questioning, she wanted me to go though some details from that night. I mean, really? I'm at work, I've already done the interview! I have to then inform my manager (who is friendly with the guy) that this would be happening,

As it went, the trains were on strike that day and he was unable to attend the interview and the police arranged with him to attend the following day. Now, if that were me, and I was being accused of a dreadful crime and was given twenty-four hours to muse over it—I am pretty sure I would have a well-considered "version of events" to present to the police. And I am pretty sure he would too. He would have had chance to come up with a story, seek advice, go through any of our correspondence on text and Facebook Messenger. A huge flaw in my opinion but the police assured me "Vic, he doesn't understand the law, this will be such a shock to him, another twenty-four hours will not change our case". I disagree actually. Strongly. She also told me how much he was "snivelling" on the phone I am still unsure why this detail was shared with me.

I was given an advocate. He was nice. It was good to sound off to someone and know he had my back. Not sure what he could actually do though really. Other than be nice. It did help to have him. I was offered counselling. But too far away for me to be able to attend and I am not to discuss any details of the incident so as to protect the case. Pretty pointless then. But thanks. I guess?

So—he denied it. I mean he would, wouldn't he? He was let

out on bail with conditions. His manager at work knows—and mine. I have to check my work calendar any time I am training in a different office to ensure our paths don't cross. So I have to keep checking his online calendar. Salt. Wound. This will never go away will it?

The IO informed me he was mortified, wouldn't stop crying. And what exactly? I have had my life torn apart, this has ruined my work life, my relationship my day to day life, my friendships, my family relationships. I am a shadow of the woman I was. His tears do not make me sympathise—is that what she was expecting of me? Who knows.

He said that he had been clear I did not want sex. He admitted that I rejected his advances at my home that night. Apparently, that doesn't matter. Nor do the dozens of messages between us where I clearly state I want a platonic friendship and do not want sex with him. That doesn't matter either. Nor do his texts afterwards saying that he knew I had been clear I did not want sex and that he was sorry I felt he took advantage and agreed that he had.

What matters, apparently, according to the IO, is that I "changed" that night. After being poured countless glasses of whisky and coke, I "changed my mind". "The situation changed". I was too inebriated to even form memories. Well lucky him then. Lucky him.

He got what he wanted and will likely get away with it. For I have little faith in the justice system. Because, it is his word against mine. He also he gets to give his version of events and let's face it could say anything he wants, not forgetting he had a good twenty-four hours to think up a nice story for the police. Twenty-four hours to prepare to answer questions. But you know, he is a man, men can't really help themselves, because as the IO pointed out, "Men are from Mars and women are from Venus". Oh. That makes it okay? She said this three times, just to make her point I guess. Not sure what her point was but to me sounds like this kind of behaviour is to be expected from blokes. And just accepted.

I still cannot believe that meeting with the IO after his arrest. I think I was there over two hours subjected to what I can only describe as a grilling. I am sure she was only ensuring we had answers for any shadows of doubt his story shed upon the allegation. Still. It pretty much felt like I was the defendant. Nice family man, clean cut, good job, nice family. While she was asking me details of some minor drug charge over twenty years ago (I am in recovery and have been for fifteen years). Of course, she implies, this may make me a less credible witness. (Are we still living in the dark ages?!)

To "corroborate" my "story" she needed to speak to a few of my friends to see if they could verify that I had "black outs" when I drank. That's pretty much the last I heard. I messaged my advocate to see if he knew what was happening. That was over a month ago. I have not had a reply. I messaged the IO to see if the file had gone off to CPS, she said it would do that week. That was that. She never bothered to let me know. Now is a waiting game.

Had it not been for the ReConnected Life group on Facebook I am not sure if I would be here to tell the tale, or if I would be sane. One thing for sure is that night I lost "me". And I will get "me" back. But it will be, and is, one hell of a struggle. The after effects of rape are long lasting. The understanding of consent seems to be vague. Like blurred lines. If a person says they do not want sex, and after a drink or two continue to say no, maybe one should take heed. Maybe you should give it up as a bad job. Do the right thing. Part company. Respect the woman. To continue plying her with booze and hoping she will change her mind, is entering into a very grey area. Drunk consent is not consent. It is rape.

I do not know what will happen to the guy who raped me. It could be a year or more before I hear. It's out of my hands. Reporting the crime was the decision I went with and the journey has been excruciating, the road to recovery arduous and slow. I can only hope that one day my smile will return as now joy is a distant memory. If this goes to court I wonder where I will find the strength to fight this battle. As that is what it has been. That is not how the justice system should be. Just too many blurred lines and as a result, broken people. I now await "justice", or at least some sort of closure.

Peace out and respect to all you survivors. Whether you reported or whether you did not.

"Victoria" xxx

NAMING IT
BY ANNA JULIET

I'm Anna. I reported sexual assault and rape (against me) in early 2017. It has been a horrendous ordeal since the perpetrator sexually assaulted me then came back and raped me in my home. I am a singer songwriter. I wrote some poems. This one, "Prayer for my Room" is about how the perpetrator violated not only me but my home. Since this I learned that the majority of rapes happen at or near the victim's home (rainn.org). Research has found that the vast majority of rapes are planned. Realising I had been set up, has been devastating. The poems touch on some of what happened when I did report this. How the myths that police are sensitive, and all have special training, from where I am standing, are actually just more myths. And then attitudes from wider community and society expands this beyond just me and my room.

I could not sleep, and people told me to go away for a while or redecorate etc.... None of these would help. I slept on the floor in the room where I was raped in my beloved music studio. My safety was shattered. I was numb. Sometimes I felt the rapist had killed me inside. I began to visualise the room as like another person, who had also been injured and needed healing. It took the guilt away from staying there and just being.... It helped me deal with this massive violation of spirit and physicality and what goes way deeper than can be explained.

This (Prayer for my Room) was the second poem I wrote after what happened. The first was a visceral account, which appears on police video. So I am not sharing it here. I will publish it later.

"I Couldn't Name it" poem three, came from the moment of taking a shower/washing over and over after the rape, while the perpetrator was still in the flat. Trying to act normal because I was so scared. It was about saying "This. is. not. happening." when it had already happened. And me, the survivor, telling myself I could stop it being rape, by not naming it. The horror of what had happened and what could unfold if I report this. Not being able to face the enormity. On your own, how can you? I said, "I'm not having this".

Realising now this was an extension of not being able to stop the rape. The freezing, even before—when you sense danger, but see no escape route. The blocking out starts during the assault. The shock and horror of the pain.... It is automatic. I had no more control over that than the sexual violence. My body tried to shut down. Trying not to feel and to rise away from the repeated hurting. When you get to the point of just waiting for it to be over. It continues through the aftermath. Intimidating masculinised police officers. All the times you were petrified into saying nothing. And being intimidated into silence, even when in the act of reporting the assault. Giving a police video when you are in fact too afraid to speak.

I lost my voice for six months. I could not sing—sometimes I could barely speak. I have had a continual sore throat. Sometimes just from having to justify myself to people patronising and talking over me. Rape is a crime of your voice being drowned out—while somebody does stuff to hurt you, he knows you did not consent and would never agree to. The perpetrator enjoyed my fear and my realisation he had trapped me. Since speaking out, my overriding experience has been of being shouted down- and spoken to as if I am a child who did something wrong, often by authorities who have a remit to help survivors. Instead you are being punished for daring to say "I". I could not bear to listen to music, let alone mix music: I went from being a productive music producer, to a little shadow.

The disregard of the police: from officers devoid of understanding, or interest to understand, what it is like to go through rape and sexual assault. The silencing never stops. "I couldn't name it" comes from being afraid to say the word "Rape" due to repercussions. From perpetrator, friends of the perpetrator and ultimately my own community. The only reason I ended up reporting, was I had injuries and had to register to get emergency meds and care e.g. the abortion pill. I would never have consented to unprotected anything, with anybody, especially not to violence, which the perpetrator inflicted. Then came fear for my safety. The horror of being told you wanted somebody to inflict injuries and swear at and degrade you while you were screaming in pain, that you would invite this type of abuse on your own body, to me is so ludicrous. I can't believe this is still said or implied to survivors.

The whole step of having to do anything about it, is life changing. You don't want that when you are feeling awful and traumatised and dishevelled after a rape. A year ago, I would never have believed at this point I could be facing a dilemma of leaving/being forced out of my home because of no longer feeling safe there. I relied on promised police safety measures (to protect from the perpetrator returning), so I could make choices, not flee out of fear.

I received bullying phone calls from police, letting me know they intend to speak to friends of the perpetrator with no assurance of my safety, obviously putting me in much more danger. Further police communications argued the perpetrator's "right" to enter my building and visit the residents complex where I live, even suggesting I move out. I was told if I encountered the perpetrator inside the building, police "hands would be tied". A disturbing email the rapist wrote within hours of assaulting me, was also ignored.

It takes time to realise not naming it, changed nothing. It still happened. Not naming it, or calling it something else is a lie. Survivors of sexual violence need support from the off, to be in a safe and confidential place to disclose and understand the enormity of what has happened, get safe medical care, a safe place to stay and take appropriate action: to be offered options. None of these were available to me.

In writing these poems and speaking out, I am naming it. We need to keep naming. By naming it now, I found other survivors. The tragedy of realising you are not alone in what you are going through, as well as the beauty and validation of meeting other courageous people prepared to stand up for our rights and stop rape culture.

If I'd had the right support upfront, one, the perpetrator might have been prevented from taking advantage when he did, and he might have been apprehended already before he even got to me. From what he said and did, he'd done it before. Two, I would have had no qualms about going straight to the police. People need support and to know their rights. In this country there is no legal representation for rape victims. You are meant to be allowed an ISVA (independent sexual violence advocate) but the waiting lists in London are over six months. The perpetrator has automatic right to a lawyer. I ended up alone in the police station. Police would not allow me to have a friend even wait for me in the building. The sexual assault centre manager, who stood up for me, had gone. The injuries the perpetrator inflicted, left me in too much pain to sit up. It was a number of days before I eventually found out where I could go to get any tests safely done. Then the sexual assault referral centre called police in. I just did not know to go there. The national rape crisis helpline constant voicemail, did not give out the number of the Havens, the suicide helpline number was on there instead. I had the most gruesome misogynistic things said to me by people on that line. I went straight to hospital after the rape and they literally ignored me every time I said, 'traumatic incident.' I was in extreme pain. and terrified. Later when I complained, there turned out to be other women's complaints who had been sexually assaulted, posted right on their website warning "do not go there if you have been sexually assaulted". The never-ending nightmare started with the first approach of the perpetrator. In fact, it started with the approach of a (female) friend of his who introduced him to me and brought him to our building and then proceeded to try to cover for him afterwards which left me feeling unspeakably betrayed. This has been one of the worst aspects. I have support from a rape support organisation who are filing a formal complaint against the police on my behalf, with direct statements from me. I am struggling to even look at the documents. My first appointment with the ISVA was this week. I was unable to read the papers in their office, as I cried all through the meeting. The case against the rapist has now been closed. I do not regret reporting. Reporting is not only about the police. It is about everybody. However appalling and unhelpful the response. I have spoken out. In making the statements, I pray I can get the words down. The pain is too much to bear. We have to turn this around. Silence keeps enabling rapists and abusers.

PRAYER FOR MY ROOM

I watch her
Violence happened here

I can't abandon her
No matter how much
I still hear her screams
No matter how much
She burns
Under the cold glare
of police neutrality
I always said I wouldn't be that girl
To beg to plead
To tell a man no, no please
There was me
All words masked by my own screams
Humiliated to the position he wanted me
A voice exploding in my head
"I did not agree!"
No words came out
He crushed my breath
With his weight
His force
His swear words
From pornography
I tried to move my hips
But he was too heavy
I lay there waiting for him to complete

So every story
has two sides
Yeah, like this one
Mine
and my room
He violated us both
Together
And one at a time

People talk of the power of rape
I want to strip that all away
Like he stripped my dignity
Long before he stripped my clothes
I couldn't see
No, the wood for the trees
Sparrow in a net
Rabbit in headlights
Caught in a machine
As he squeezed me through
Unmoved by my pain
And hers
No clichés no words like these express
My fear, terror
Hopelessness

One girl is not enough
It would take a posse of women
To heal this
All with real powers
Like witches
They could take us
Burn us at the stake, yes
Steal our herbs away
Replace them with pharmacy
Masculinity
Penises cast in stone
The injuries he caused
Leaving me to feel like
Jelly and bone
As my body wastes away
I cling to life

By telephone cord
And dull-lit screen
Since no friends wanna come round any more
Afraid to be faced with true life catastrophe
When in reality it's just one girl tryin' to heal

My room is like a quiet woman
She hangs her head in shame
Trying to make sense
Of the pornographic storm
That shattered her face
Invisible
But for a few stains
After some kind of a bomb went off here

Still I watch her
Still she grieves
Silently she weeps
No one sees

I couldn't leave her
Just like one bereaved
I curl up by her belly
And I try to sleep

Can I hope to
Console her?

So many wakeful nights
No need for CCTV
The whole horror show
Plays inside of me

The ultimate control
If he could
Impregnate me

I woke up and it was spring
Daffodils are blooming
Last time I looked it was cold
It was new year
It was January
My clock stopped there
Now it's too hot
For my too many clothes
I'm lost
I'm still picking up stuff
Dropped on the floor
That night
No one knows
The grief my cries
For those missing months
My Time
Gone forever
Together with the parts of me
They scraped away
In the gynae suite

Please
Stop tellin' me, try therapy
Yes
What d'ya know
I did that already
Stop throwing me futile leads
Some things
Are deeper than that

This wound is more than a gash
In our background
Of rape culture
New men like vultures
Circling for prey
When they hear what happened
It's not your fault
They say
Who'll be the first
To call me a liar
Whore
Bitch
Traitor
I heard all these pointless words before
I heard them in my head again
Before you ever said them this time
I already made my decision
To speak out about this crime
You ignored my 'no '
When you set up the justice system
Just so

Guys
I don't see you in the streets
At parliament
Protesting my rights
No matter
How much your handwringing afterwards
Yet you say you care
While wanting to assert your
Domination everywhere

I pray for my room

I pray for the law
I don't pray for your souls
No
I don't forgive you
While you still make me live this
Put us thru
This Hell on earth
I don't pray to your god
I pray to my own
I reject your useless angels
And suggestions to do meditation
To go away for the weekend
As if that
Would solve anything

Rearranging the furnishings
Replacing bedding
And redecorating
After rape
Did not remove his and all the other men's hate
And the memories I can't erase
Too traumatised to go to bed or take a shower
As it reminds me of that morning after when I stayed there for
an hour
Washing myself
Washing myself
Over and over
No tears,
Not like in the movies
They took a month to come
Crying 'til I'm numb
Now they wash my face
Until it Runs

You never heard sobs
And wails like this one

Sometimes the tears fall silently
But they're always there
Like under the bright light
Of the police statement room
It went out
As in a power cut
"It's movement sensitive"
The detective said
It could not detect life in that room
You were laid down so still
Talking in a whisper
With your eyes closed
The policewoman was concentrating
So she forgot to move her arm
It all went dark
Stopped your words that came right out of your heart
It happens, he said.
Always I noticed at the crucial moment though

So I froze
Just like in the rape
I didn't shed a tear for four hours
No break
I broke down in the control room after they turn off the tape
Two police stare
"Why are you crying?" they say
Oblivious
Like they don't care
I apologise for taking up space
I pull myself together

Stop telling me "it'll be okay—"
"It's good to let it all out"
Stop telling me
What this is about
While you reap the spoils
Strut and swagger
Raise your shouts
To drown out my whisper
Now my voice is almost lost
I realise what it was for
I recognise the cost
I pray
For so much more

I COULDN'T NAME IT

I couldn't name it
The enormity of the act
Putting it back
To erase
Block
Stopping it
After it was
Already too late

I couldn't control
It on the night
But afterwards
I, wanting to deny

If I could make it go away
By washing

Saying nothing
Speak in anonymity
To try to heal just me

Afterwards
Showering
This
Is
Not
Happening

Panicking
In silence
Understanding
His pain
Making
His mental state
The reason
Like an accident
Unforeseen
A thunderstorm
In a tea cup
Somebody to tell me
It was nothing
Is all I seek

The enormity
Brutality
Violence
Already buried
Deep in me
In my shattered room
My heart

My womb
Which he wanted to impregnate
And did not bleed again
Since that day

The real name for this act
I could not say
The truth about my pain
My shame
That
I never wanted
to acknowledge
He did this
To me

He was
Cold as ice
I was petrified
He ignored my cries
He knew his needs
He meant it
Every step
Every thrust

I said I didn't
Want sex
I said I said
Said it again
He says
Yes
I know
I should have been
more careful

I didn't realise
what was at stake
It took a long time
to get going
cos of your pain
Still
I could not find a name
for my heart ache

This violence
Violation
Pornographic
Attack
Soul level
Hurt my whole
Tiny sensitivity
Trashed smashed
And left to bleed
It's like he wanted to kill
What is inside me

Not put off by my screams
Not really
His erection
Tells me everything
Like coke and Viagra
In his blood stream
Going going going
And going
No mercy or compassion
He drains all of hers
Sadistic pleasure
In her devastation

Makin' it her duty
To make him come

Afterwards when he
Left her home
He says he'll stop it now
To protect us both
To protect himself later
He knows his own danger
His rage
Only matched by his anger
When she took the morning after pill
She was at the hospital
His momentary terror
When he realises he might be
Called out on his behaviour
Arrested for

Quickly superseded by swagger
And arrogance
He doesn't even ask
For a lawyer
So sure he can blag
Lie
Bullshit
And talk his way out of the corner
The police recorder no bother

He knows
Only the women get
Accused of lying
He's still laughing

She's still grieving
Her insides still bleeding
Stomach still heaving
Spine burning
Throat rasping
She lost her appetite
Since that night

She never goes out
She just avoids
Her voice drowned out
In all the noise
Rape is a crime of choice
Vs no choice
It is not a story with two equal sides
It's a violation of rights

It is an act of premeditation
Not a misunderstanding of a situation
He did not misread a signal
He knew full well.
Before
After
During
Still

He manipulated his way in
He'll manipulate his way out
It takes a real skill
To see what this is about

In the intoxication
Of waiting for something so long

You can overlook things that are wrong

Don't be fooled
Friends, family
And boys in blue
Don't leave him
Laughing at you

I couldn't name it
Still no words
To express this
Terrified of pressing charges
Being called a bitch
Yet being told if he does it again on your head be it
Petrified of inciting
His wrath
Perhaps that of neighbours too
I fell into the compassion trap
Then to be humiliated
By rape interview
They say no man never admits to
What were you wearing?
You wouldn't believe they still
Ask these questions
The WPC made me say penis
On video
Like otherwise it's not true
Just in case you weren't sure about my humiliation
Now you knew
Better than his letter
Abandoning me to a
Living death, yes—
They dismiss my trauma

Casually as ordering extra croutons
Couldn't name it
Some of the reasons

WALL OF SILENCE

We don't have to look to ISIS
Nor Al Qaeda
The crisis is right here
Stop silencing
Stop the gas-lighting
Stop denying my
experience
this very existence
Stop the hate
You rape
Then say it's nothing
Laws all made by men
Privileging men
black, white and brown
Stop calling me a whore
Just for speaking out
Stop punishing me
Saying I can't be believed
Stop ostracising me
You listen only to your own police
I have no ally in this band of thieves
You attack my femininity like I'm the
Original Eve

Take from me then deny it ever
belonged to me you claim I gave
freely when you heard my screams

You say it was my fantasy when
you saw me bleed
You felt my tears
She who was in your dreams
You plotted and schemed to trap
me then attack me you covered your tracks
Desperate so you can say
She retracted her story
No she did not and she never will
This is not a story it is factual
It is not an allegation it's
A report

You think the only thing that counts is court
Laughing with your
jury of peers
who cover their ears
Burden of proof to
Fall always on the daughters
You so comfortable here
Don't even ask for
Your designated lawyer
There was never one for her
You know the only protection
was for the perpetrator
Think you'll intimidate me
With your silence and sneers
Your anti-woman jeers
Consent is not fear
It is not intimidation
It is not trapping someone into a situation
It is not pretending to have a close relation
It is not your own alcohol and substance inebriation

Bet You didn't put yourself in that altered state
To plead your innocence at the police station

Consent is not
alone,
Kind,
Sorry for you
It is not
me saying no
While you perpetrate what you want regardless
It is not taking a kind caring woman
And calling her a ho
You knew it was no
It is not inventing anything you can to make it not so
You, twice my weight, twice my size
Dead weight on my hips
I could not prise
Stop the lies
Like the whole world is your ally

I decide
what I want
Not you
Not him
Not that man there
Not that woman who said
'He's always been alright with me
He is like my brother'
This is my Body
I decide
I was clear
You are not welcome here
You never were

Intruder in my room pushed your way in
Stop wrapping up your fears and
Blaming it on her
You are responsible
You made a choice
It is not a case of boys will be boys
You do not get to drown out my voice

That a man should be held accountable
for damage he's done
Is this too much to ask?
I'm tearing down your rapist's mask
This wall of silence
You throw in my face
Like the bloody insult you are
You all collude
Enable
Complicit you
This despicable crime
You carry out
Behind closed doors
Or in full view
Then walk away
And say it wasn't you
It was you
You knew then
Know now
Stand up
Be a man
Hold up your hands
Acknowledge your violence

TESTIMONY OF A SILENCED SURVIVOR

RAPE

On 23rd November 2011 I was sitting in a criminal law lecture, covering sexual offences.

The Sexual Offences Act 2003 defines rape as the penile penetration of the vagina, anus or mouth without reasonable belief in consent. Consent is legally defined as *agreeing by choice* and having the *freedom* and *capacity* to make that choice.

It was the capacity element that awakened me. An individual does not have capacity, and therefore cannot consent, if they were asleep or otherwise unconscious at the time of the relevant act.

I realised at that moment that I had been raped.

SILENCED

I was repeatedly raped from July 2007 until August 2008. I knew I had not consented and there was no way he could have reasonably believed that I was consenting. Yet, at the time, I was unable to name my experiences as rape.

I was, however, very open about what was happening to me with those around me. I would say "he was trying to have sex with me while I was asleep". Yet no one else named my experiences as rape either.

When I challenged him with "What you are doing to me is *like* rape", he repeatedly said "No it's not. You are *my* wife." and "Anyway, I am more intelligent than *you!*".

I was constantly second guessing myself; I knew it was wrong, it felt wrong, but I was not being heard or validated.

It would take me nearly six years to speak out.

VALIDATION

Despite the fact that I was able to name what happened to me in the context of a criminal law lecture, at that stage, reporting to the police did not cross my mind. It took me a long time to process the reality of my experiences, from which I had spent years dissociating.

During my study of law, I was gifted with a life-changing friendship. Deborah was the first person who really *heard* me and *chose* to enter my world and be alongside me. She created a safe space for me to open up to her, to explore those painful memories and feelings. When I did, Deborah believed me. She gently challenged my self-blame and the myths I held; my experiences were truly validated.

It was our relationship that enabled me to come to terms with having been raped; I did that at my own pace, in my own time, nearly two years after that criminal law lecture.

RESPONSIBILITY

Realising I was raped brought with it an overwhelming sense of responsibility to other women.

I knew he had never taken responsibility for raping me. He thought it his God-given right; he not only told me so but had continued to rape me, again and again, despite my cries. I *knew* he'd do it again to other women and this preoccupied me for a long time.

I wasn't sure how to resolve the discomfort this knowledge brought me until one day in May 2013 when I was told that another woman made a sexual assault "allegation" against him. I *knew* he was guilty, but the police decided to take no further action.

I felt responsible; if I had reported that I had been raped perhaps that would have deterred him from sexually assaulting her, or any other woman. Thankfully I had Deborah alongside me, helping to shift the blame to him.

I knew that I had to do something. Not just for myself but for her and for all women.

THE FIRST BARRIER TO JUSTICE

I made an informed decision to report. I explored my options and the potential impacts of reporting with the National Rape Crisis Helpline and with Deborah. I also knew, through my study of law and from the media, the appalling way in which women who report are treated. Nevertheless, I was determined to proceed. I was telling the truth. I had done nothing wrong. Surely I was deserving of the protection of the law?

I called ahead and made an appointment to report to a Sexual Offences Investigative Trained (SOIT) officer. However, on arrival at the police station, I was met with a male police officer that had little skill or sensitivity. He was the first barrier to me accessing justice.

He demanded to know the details of what I intended to report. I expressed my preference not to discuss the details of my experiences at the reception of a police station. He responded, "Well, I need to know because if it was just the touching of the boob or something, then they won't come down to see you, they expect us to take the report".

Yes, he *really* said that. And, of course, Deborah was my witness.

With Deborah alongside me, together we were able to challenge his minimisation of women's traumatic experiences, inappropriateness and lack of awareness. Had Deborah not been there, I may well have walked out.

We waited for quite some time while uniform and the Sapphire Unit argued about which department's responsibility it was to take the initial report. There was no consideration for my interests, nor how their transparent passing of the buck was affecting me. The Sapphire Unit, the department with officers specially trained in sexual violence, won the battle. A female officer from uniform took the report from me.

My case was then passed on to the Sapphire Team and only then did a SOIT officer meet with me, briefly. She spoke to me with disdain and left me wishing she hadn't even bothered. I had to challenge the way she spoke to me before she began to take me seriously, and treat me with any shred of respect.

I felt exhausted. Was I going to have to fight throughout this entire process to be treated with respect, like a human being?

TRUSTING THE 'JUSTICE' SYSTEM

In July 2013, after I had given my full statement via pre-recorded video evidence, the SOIT officer notified me that the Crown Prosecution Service (CPS) had decided to charge my ex-husband with seven accounts of rape against me. I was conflicted; I felt relieved and yet was riddled with anxiety.

I was told to expect a call from the police the day after his arrest. The call never came. Despite my efforts, I could not contact anyone who could confirm whether he was still in custody, had been remanded, bailed, or released. It was four days until the Officer in Charge (OIC) of the case, would be back in the office. I spent that entire time on edge, looking over my shoulder.

When I eventually received the call, I was informed he had been remanded until the Plea and Case Management Hearing (PCMH). Not because an allegation of rape was made against him and he was a danger to society but because he was an over-stayer found in possession of two fake European passports; he was a flight risk.

The OIC told me how significant it was that I had come forward to report, "I want you to know that there will never, ever, be a question of whether or not you are telling the truth. As you know, he has done exactly the same thing to another woman; he used exactly the same modus operandi".

Let me break that down.

"There will never, ever, be a question of whether or not you are telling the truth".

Excuse me, why would there be?

"As you know, he has done exactly the same thing to another woman; he used exactly the same modus operandi".

Well actually, no, I didn't know that. I was told that he had sexually assaulted another woman; I did not know that he had raped her, or that he had done so in exactly the same way he raped me, while she was asleep. That information took me back to my own experience. It cut deep, as though I had been cut with a knife.

I was informed that as a result of me coming forward an application would be made to the CPS for the other survivor's case to be reopened.

The OIC assured me that he would do everything in his power to investigate and present a case that would secure a conviction. He further assured me that, even if a conviction could not be secured, at least he would be deported from the UK; he was an over-stayer facing conviction of possessing false travel documents. I was reassured that either way, I wouldn't have to live in fear worrying about his whereabouts.

At that moment I placed my full trust in the OIC, in the Metropolitan Police, and in the criminal justice system more broadly. I had a romanticised notion that the criminal justice system was a 'justice' system.

RE-VICTIMISATION AND BROKEN TRUST

The Plea and Case Management Hearing (PCMH) took place three months after he was arrested.

I was not allowed to attend this court hearing myself, as it would have potentially prejudiced the proceedings. However, I sensed that I needed someone there on my behalf, someone I could trust. The SOIT officer would be attending and assured me she would report everything back to me. Despite the fact our relationship had improved from our first meeting, I would never place my trust in her; she had shown me who she was when we first met. I decided to ask a friend to sit in the public gallery to ensure that I was kept fully in the loop.

My friend, Kim, kindly took the day off work. I drove her from London to the hearing, a two-hour drive away and I kept myself busy in the shops while the hearing was taking place; trying not to think about what was happening.

Kim sat in the public gallery with three young girls who were observing court proceedings during half-term. Before the judge had entered the courtroom and before the hearing had begun, Kim overheard a conversation between the prosecution barrister, SOIT officer, and CPS representative. Of particular note from their conversation was the following:

"*Maybe she should have just stayed in Harlesden*", "*No she shouldn't, she shouldn't have started a law degree"*.

Laughter followed these statements.

Kim was in shock at what she had heard. After all, the defence barrister and the defendant were present in the courtroom at the time, and would also have heard the conversation. For the duration of the hearing she was completely consumed with thoughts of how she would tell me how 'professionals', who were supposedly on my side, had spoken about me in a public courtroom.

He entered a plea of not guilty.

When Kim delivered this news, I was floored. It was a double blow. He entered a not guilty plea. Further, any trust I had in the police and prosecution was broken; I had been re-victimised by them.

Kim and I discussed these words at length after the hearing (incidentally, while we were waiting for a tow truck to take us back to London). Her first-hand impressions aligned with mine; namely, that what she overheard in court amounted to victim blaming.

Firstly, if it hadn't been for me, the fact that I left Harlesden, then I wouldn't have met him, and therefore wouldn't have been raped.

Secondly, if it hadn't been for me, a girl from Harlesden (a socioeconomically deprived area of London), educating myself, then I would have never understood that what had happened to me was rape. I would never have reported, and they wouldn't be sitting in a courtroom having to deal with this case.

The very people who are supposed to be representing the interests of survivors, a police officer specially trained in sexual offences and the prosecution, were laughing at me, and blaming me for the fact that they were all sat there in court, and worse, they were blaming me for the fact that I was raped! Even if they hadn't all spoken the words, every one of them was complicit in their silence, failure to challenge, and worse, their validating laughter.

Again, my trust was broken. I was being re-victimised by the very system that was supposed to be fighting for justice for me.

I knew then I was going to have to keep fighting throughout the entire process, to be respected and to be treated as a human being; and that I did.

Looking back, I wonder how I had the strength to do so. I guess I went into survival mode; the only chance I had at achieving justice was by fighting for it myself. Thus, I advocated on my own behalf to the police, and as a result, the SOIT officer and prosecution barrister were removed from the case. A new SOIT officer was allocated and the CPS instructed a new barrister to represent the prosecution.

MY TRIAL

The first time I met the new prosecution barrister was the first day of the trial; she too treated me with disdain. After making it clear that she was not representing me, but the State, she asked if I had any questions. The questions I asked were met with a tone and response that made me feel ignorant, as though I should have known the answers. She ordered me not to mention the other survivor, as this would result in a mistrial and that *she* didn't want that.

If I didn't know it already, I knew there and then, my interests were invisible.

On the second day of the trial I was called as a witness for the prosecution. My pre-recorded evidence was played, after which I was cross-examined from behind a screen.

I managed to hold it together up until the moment I stepped foot in the courtroom. I began shaking. I felt as though I was in a daze; it was an out of body experience. As I opened my mouth to swear the oath, I felt as though the words would not come out. But somehow, I composed myself and reached deep for my inner strength.

I was subjected to a fierce and aggressive cross-examination; I was called a liar and accused of acting. The defence barrister was a bully; he was shouting at me, badgering me, and had hatred in his eyes.

He was so relentless that, at one point, the judge had to intervene. It felt as though I was the one on trial. It was extremely traumatic, and I was left feeling numb.

Deborah was also called as a witness for the prosecution, as she had played such an important role in witnessing the realisation I had been raped. By this stage, any trust I had in the criminal (in)justice system had already been taken from me. Therefore, after she gave evidence, she offered to sit in on the remainder of the trial, to be my eyes and ears.

As the trial unfolded, it became clear that there were inadequacies in the police investigation, which had resulted in a potential prosecution witness refusing to give evidence and another switching from a prosecution witness to a defence witness. There were also issues of police (mis)conduct that had the potential to affect the case.

Once again, no one was advocating for my interests, and the prosecution did not have the commitment and passion to challenge the lies put forward by the defence.

The police recommended that I return to court for the judge's summing up to the jury, to provide me with some closure, in the event of a not guilty verdict.

As I walked into the public gallery, I immediately began to question whether I made the right decision. A member of the jury pointed me out to a fellow juror. She seemed shocked to see me back in court. When I sat down to my left there was only frosted glass between my ex-husband and me; I felt sick.

Although I cannot recall the words the judge used in any detail, they had a profound impact on me. I *knew* that she believed me, inherently. Surely the jury would too?

SILENCED, *AGAIN*

It was the matter of a few hours, two or three at the most, and the verdict was in. Deborah and I rushed back to the court. As we approached the court, I recognised a juror walking out of the building. I knew at that moment what the verdict was.

Deborah told me to wait down the road while she ran in to find out the verdict. Something in me was still holding out a little bit of hope.

I saw her come running out of the building towards me. She didn't say anything, but I *knew*. I collapsed onto the pavement and let out an almighty scream; I wailed uncontrollably, while Deborah held me.

I felt an excruciating pain; I had been silenced, once again.

THE *OTHER SURVIVOR'S* TRIAL

Despite the fact that I was devastated by the not guilty verdict, there was still hope that he would be convicted of raping the other survivor, and for the meantime, he was still on remand so posed no threat to us or any other woman.

As a result of me reporting, the police were able to appeal to the CPS, to re-open the other survivor's case. The appeal was initially refused, on the basis that the CPS believed that the "The two complainants have conspired, together, against the suspect".

I didn't even know her name, so the suggestion that I conspired with her was ludicrous, and not grounded in any evidence. Which is ironic given that the CPS is supposed to make decisions to charge suspects on the basis of evidence.

The police then appealed to the Director of Public Prosecutions (DPP), and finally, some procedural justice was achieved; the other survivor would also get her day in court. At that stage, there was still the hope that the two cases would be heard together.

However, the hope of a joined trial was shattered soon after. At a pre-trial hearing, the judge refused the application on the basis "It would be prejudicial to the defendant to join the two cases, as they are completely different, one woman was married to the defendant, the other was not".

I was confused to say the very least. The marital rape exemption, on the basis of supposed 'implied consent,' was abolished in R v R (1991). Twenty-three years on, and a Crown Court judge believed that rape within marriage was somehow different to rape outside of marriage? This just goes to show how deeply entrenched rape myths are.

Five months after the first trial, he was also found not guilty of raping the other survivor.

Further injustice.

I truly empathised with her; I knew exactly how she must have felt.

To this day I don't know her name. I only hope that she is living well, and has found some peace.

A *LEGAL* WHITEWASH

After the PCMH the OIC was permitted to listen to the court recording of my re-victimisation at the PCMH. He told me that the conversation was completely inappropriate and warranted a formal complaint, and promised to help me obtain the recording after the trial.

After the trial, I submitted formal complaints to the police,

CPS and Bar Standards Board, the regulatory body for barristers.

During the complaint processes, I attempted to obtain a recording or a transcript of the conversation that took place at the PCMH. The police refused to assist me as promised and I felt as though they had abandoned me, washed their hands of me. All the promises for on-going support afterward came to nothing. I had served my purpose.

The same judge who believed that marital rape was different to non-marital rape refused to provide me with the recording. The Bar Standards Board then submitted a request, which was also refused.

Around that time, I remember a family friend, who investigates complaints at a regulatory body, saying something along the lines of "When you are making a complaint to so many different agencies, you have to ask yourself whether they are the problem, or if, in fact, you are".

I reflected upon what she said, for a second. But then my sense of what is right, what is fair, and what is just, kicked in; of course, I wasn't the problem, they were.

The responses I received to each of my complaints were that the conduct of the individuals involved did not amount to a breach of professional standards; it was a legal whitewash.

Yet another injustice I was forced to swallow.

A SMALL SENSE OF JUSTICE

After the trial, I made an application to the Criminal Injuries Compensation Authority for compensation.

Initially, my application was refused on the basis that I hadn't applied within their time limit (two years from the date the crime took place). This time limit directly discriminates against survivors of sexual violence, as it widely known that many take years to come to terms with, let alone report, what happened to them; and I had provided evidence from psychotherapists to that effect.

Knowing how unjust this decision was, I applied for a reconsideration of the decision and challenged the discriminatory nature of this rule and the decision maker's lack of understanding of sexual violence.

Finally, on the application for reconsideration, I was granted compensation. While money has not, nor ever will, compensate for the fact that I was repeatedly raped for over a year, the award of compensation provided some validation of what happened to me.

I had, *finally*, been believed.

A *small* sense of justice.

AND STILL I RISE

All of this happened over the final year of my law degree. The trial itself happened two weeks before my final exams. I am not quite sure how I did it, but I was not going allow him to take another thing from me, and he didn't. I managed to get through it all and achieve a First Class Honours Degree.

Despite this enormous achievement, my treatment within the criminal (in)justice system shattered my career plans. I had been offered a place starting the Bar Professional Training Course in September 2014 and had received a scholarship from one of the Inns of Court. However, the very 'justice' system that I was striving to work within had re-victimised me, I didn't receive procedural justice, let alone justice in the form of a guilty verdict; I was silenced once again. My aspiration of becoming a criminal law barrister was no longer; I couldn't conscionably be a part of an unjust system.

Notwithstanding these many injustices, in the words of Maya

Angelou, "still I rise". I may have been victimised, repeatedly, but I am, after all, a *Survivor*, albeit a silenced[1] one.

I am currently undertaking a Masters in Woman and Child Abuse, and am volunteering within the sexual violence support sector. I am committed to utilising my knowledge, skills and experience to support other survivors of sexual violence through the criminal (in)justice system.

---

[1] The Criminal (In)Justice System continues to silence me. I am unable to attach my name to this chapter for fear of a libel case being brought against me; after all he was found not guilty. However, other than changing my friends' names to protect myself from potential legal action, nothing contained within this chapter amounts to a false statement.

PERMISSION TO SPEAK... DENIED
BY YVONNE MICHÈLE

I was eleven. My Mum had passed away on Mother's Day; I was totally distraught. It started three days after her passing. He was my cousin and it carried on for about eighteen months; it stopped because my family were evicted from our home.

I hadn't even had any conversations about boyfriends, men, puberty, periods much less sex!

I felt scared, I felt ashamed about it, I felt dirty, I didn't know why I felt that way, I didn't know how it was wrong, but it felt wrong. It confused me. He told me; made me promise not to tell anyone ...it was our little secret .... I didn't tell anyone, I never spoke about it, I struggled with it, was it okay to be touched that way, was it okay for him to put his 'bits' in me...I pushed every unpleasant thought to the furthest darkest crevice in the back of my mind; even when I was violently sick at the thought, I kept the secret to myself.

In 2012, I'd started to look at self-development. It was becoming increasingly difficult to hide my shame and live with me.

A client in the salon where I worked asked me outright, had I ever been abused? I was horrified and got defensive at the time, she said she could tell by my behaviour! She told me that it was not too late to do something about it ... Her words were ringing in my head.

I'm forty-eight now, and I reported it four years ago in 2013. I didn't think I could as so many years had passed....

I'm active in my church, and had been appointed to be a safeguarding officer within the church and so I'd had some training for that role. I started to find out about how to protect and safeguard vulnerable peopled and how easily things can get swept under the carpet.

The Jimmy Saville scandal was unfolding in the news, other vulnerable women within the church were disclosing to me in my role as safeguarding officer; I found myself advising them, helping them and yet not helping myself or taking my own advice.

Even though I had pushed what had happened to me to the back of my mind, working in this field began to trigger old memories. I realised that even though decades had passed it had slowly been eating away at the core of my soul. I realised that the action I had taken to protect myself was destroying the very essence of who I was. I was so angry, bitter and riddled in so much emotional pain, the silence was destroying me.

It was all too much for me, it felt like all the unspoken words, unspoken emotions, unspoken feelings were lodged in the centre of my throat and was about to suffocate me, I needed to release myself from this invisible bondage, I needed to speak, I needed to tell someone, but I didn't know how. I was so scared; I was petrified about what people would think of me ...what they would say ... would they even believe me... how they would look at me.

Eventually, I found the courage to speak to another safeguarding professional and in that conversation, I told her what had happened to me. She was kind and understanding, telling the truth wasn't as bad as I had imagined, she asked me what I wanted to do. Part of me wanted to talk about it openly, but another part of me wanted to run and hide.

When I was ready, she stayed with me. I made the call, the appointment was made, she came with me, we went to the police station. It was a female police officer, I was thankful for that, she was easy to talk to talk to, I made my statement, and I've no complaints about her.

Words are hard to find about how I felt at that time. Essentially, I regressed back to my eleven-year old self. Constantly in tears I could feel all the emotions I had tried so hard to forget and not feel.

I became that child again for a long period of time. Reporting it brought back so much of the old memories that I didn't want to remember, the pain, the fear, the shame but there was nowhere to put it, nowhere to store it, I had to face it!

I felt like I'd lost my mind...

I wasn't functioning. I was numb. I was just going from day to day. I was beginning to realise that I hadn't accepted it and it was choking me. From the moment I opened my mouth and told the truth of what had happen to me it started to release the poison that had built up for thirty odd years. The residue of all of those moments was slowly departing. I'm convinced that's why as an adult I've not been unable to settle in any relationship, with people in general, I've not been able to trust fully.

I thought that once I was interviewed once that would be all that was required, but there was more than one interview, and all recorded with the camera set up. The police asked the questions, and they probed until they got all the evidence they needed.

I felt like I was on that witness stand already. I felt I had to prove it. It felt like I was on trial. It felt as though I was pleading with somebody to believe me. I felt demoralized and unworthy. I wished I had never said a word, I felt so small.

Having to go through that process as an adult is very

challenging, I don't know how a child would go through it!

I tried to remember everything, I was having flashbacks, my brain did not work in sequence, sporadic random images would appear in my mind. I felt under pressure to remember every last detail. It was definitely traumatising to relive it over and over again, in detail. In my mind I had thought that I could just say what happened and walk away. I was wrong!

The flashbacks and the nightmares were disabling. I was waking up in cold sweats, I felt nauseous, I had ulcers in my mouth and a sty on my eyes because of the amount of stress I was under. The trauma of it became a constant thing. It's like you're sitting on a rapidly moving merry-go-round, you feel constantly sick, but you can't get off, and it just keeps spinning.

The police advised me not to talk about it with anyone. I became very isolated because of that. I couldn't even have a conversation with my own sister. Again, I was silenced. When I came back from the police, I could only tell my family that the police would be paying them a visit in regard to me; I wasn't allowed to discuss anything. I assured my family that I hadn't done anything wrong, and that the police were going to ask them some questions about me.

I felt totally isolated in every way. I'm the victim, I was the child. Still, thirty years later, nothing changes. Invisible, the little girl that sits in the corner crying so much, she has no eyes and she has no voice. Silenced.

Victim support was offered. I went a couple of times. It was a complete waste of my time. They're volunteers, they meant well, they're not equipped to deal with what was happening, it was awkward.

I started having counselling later on, through a private organisation, The Hope Foundation. But they had a quota of only six sessions. I had those sessions way before the court. One day after having a flashback I needed somebody to talk to and called I was told I couldn't speak to anyone and that my sessions had come to an end ...I totally lost it! That day was one of my darkest days ever and to be told I had to just deal with it wasn't going to work for me. I was so distraught I could hardly speak. I was relentless, I demanded to see someone and said If I don't make it till tomorrow it will be on your head! I received a call from the chief executive from the organisation, she had overheard the conversation and told the receptionist to call me back. She gave me an additional twelve weeks of counselling.

Who says twelve sessions is enough?

But it would have to do.

I had a breakdown that day, I didn't know it at the time. I just know I wasn't coping. I'll never forget that day. I could literally see the eleven-year-old me sitting under a wash basin in the corner of a room sobbing and just didn't know what to do with myself!

There was no-one to talk to. Everyone that I could have talked to was part of the trial, and I had already been told I wasn't allowed. It may jeopardise the case!

I was so low. I definitely needed the therapy, I don't think I would have made it without it.

The fact I'd started on my self-development journey was a huge help. I coached myself. I learnt some tools to help my coping mechanism. Taking small steps each day to make myself function, being a mum and having a business were all a combined catalyst to keep going, keep working. I would have lost my home and much more if I hadn't learnt the techniques of how to reframe things and use it on a daily basis.

Two and a half years is a long time to wait for a court date. It's like being at the same funeral for two and a half years, the same songs, the same bible readings, the same coffin, the same people crying, the same funeral service. It was a black time. There was no colour. The only little light was the anticipation of the day to come, and that was all there was. I just had to wait!

The CPS had said it would take six to nine months to go to trial... two and a half years later we were still waiting for a date. Out of my control there was nothing I could do to change or make this process move faster.

Imagine being on the biggest rollercoaster, with no seatbelt, in complete darkness and you can't see where you're going, you can only feel the dry air around you, and hear the whispers in the darkness, you feel it go to another level, yet you have no strength or energy. It's another day but your still in darkness your stomach is just going up and down, beads of sweat drip down your forehead, you panic for no reason; every day. Then you get to what feels like the pinnacle....

Yes! This is the day. It's going to be this date in November 2014. Then, to be told ...it's not, it's not going to be until next year, not until February....

It was the scariest, loneliest time I've ever experienced. I have lost many dear friends and gone through that grief, but at least I could talk to someone, at least there is an outlet to help ease the pain, but there was no communication except the counsellor which was once a fortnight. It felt like I was in prison and I wasn't allowed any visitors. Even some of my friends who were there with me in the beginning disappeared.

I did not connect with myself or ask myself how I really felt about it all?

These feelings were all new to me, confusing me but I just had to be patient with myself, nurture myself. I had to learn to be kind to myself, and give myself time.

The trial was in February 2015 and lasted a week.

The fact that my case was actually going to trial was a massive boost for me. I had been told a lot of cases don't go to trial. To me it meant that someone believed me. It meant that going through the trauma of flashbacks, nightmares and what I call a 'breakdown' was all worth it!

Perpetrators make their victims believe that no-one will believe you. They put doubt in your mind... I remember seeing him in a car park before the trial and he stood right in front of my car, if I had driven I would have run him over (the thought did cross my mind) he just snarled at me, he intimidated me, and I froze ...

I was scared of him and what he might do.

Questions would always plague my mind... Why didn't I say anything at the time? Because I couldn't. I felt like I didn't have permission.

That week of the trial, nothing would stay in my stomach. I felt physically sick every day. I felt like I was going to have a heart attack every moment, my heart was pounding too quickly. I was in constant panic. Holding my breath. Head is light. Dizzy. Scared. Petrified at what was about to happen.

I have faith. I believe in Jesus Christ. Yet I had no support from my local church that I had served in but that did not deter my faith. I knew I was alone on this rollercoaster. No-one was sitting next to me. There was no seat belt. Nothing to hold me, or reassure me, just my faith.

When I gave my evidence, I was advised to do it behind a curtain so only the jury could see me. This one thing is my biggest regret.

I wish to God that I had faced him. Looked him right in his eyes and told of his perversion. Using that screen did not help me or the case at all.

I was seated first, then the jury walked in as soon as I saw them my heart sank, I knew it wasn't going to go well. **Eleven** of the jury were **men**. Only one woman, who was a white. Ten white men. One Asian man. That is not a balanced jury. I am a black woman.

You would think that with twenty-first century demographics, the jury would have looked somewhat different and would have reflected a more diverse selection of people. The age range also looked alike, they all looked like they were in their early forties. All the men looked the same, with their big bellies they looked like clones.

The CPS who were representing me spent less than five minutes with me before the trial started, they didn't really explain anything to me; the police officer was changed at the last moment because the female officer who had taken the statements had since moved to another area and he wasn't helpful either. Again, silenced and isolated.

Finding your own legal team would be of more benefit.

I was then informed after giving evidence by the police and the court workers that I couldn't go into the courtroom because I had given evidence from behind the screen and that I would have to go home and wait it out. *[Editor's note: not actually true, but it is dissuaded and often that's what the witness is made to think.]* Again, I was isolated from the whole case. It felt like someone had taken a samurai sword (like in the film Kill Bill) and cut my head off. I had to go home and wait. Thursday, they said. No-one called. Friday came. I'm calling. No-one told me anything. The verdict had been given.

There was a different police officer, a male officer, who'd been assigned to my case. With him, there was no bonding. He had just turned up at court, telling me that he'd be my officer. I felt anxious about this but there was no-one for me to tell. Eventually after calling all afternoon and into the evening he answered my call and told me, the verdict...

NOT GUILTY!

He's been found not guilty. He went on to say that the verdict doesn't mean he's not guilty it just means there was not enough evidence.

My heart felt like it stopped. The words were jumbled in my head, how can this be....

Broken, disappointed, confused and I put the phone down and fell to the floor.

The words of the police officer kept ringing in my head: the verdict doesn't mean he's not guilty it just means there was not enough evidence....

What a load of bullshit! WE all know that the law says, 'innocent until proven guilty.' So, in the eyes of the law, **he's innocent**. I felt that lump reappear in my throat again. I found it hard to say the words...

HE IS GUILTY!

Today he is working around vulnerable young people, elderly people; he still has access to them. I feel like my hands have been cut off, my mouth bound up. I still can't talk about it as he was found not guilty.

I have to set myself free. I have to defy what I have been told.

Even writing this, I'm not supposed to say who I am. I am supposed to write this anonymously but what he fails to realise is I've been fighting all my life, I've been fighting to find my voice, I've been fighting to be who I am... and this is a fight that I will win!

How the hell is anything going to change if I don't speak? How the hell is something going to change if I continue to do what I've always done?

If I don't speak out, others will never know, and it will remain a secret. There are young people out there who have been affected right now and are afraid to speak, there are women and men who have carried their abuse for years, ashamed of what happened to them and unless they hear someone else's story they might not have the courage to speak out for themselves. They tell me I'm not allowed to speak like I'm supposed to wait to get permission?

The word Allow means something different to me now. I can't allow this to go on any more. I will not allow vulnerable people to be put at risk while I have breath in my body.

I am not asking for permission to speak; I am not asking permission to tell my own story... I am serving notice... I will not be silenced anymore!

My recovery has been slow, but it has been thorough. I know myself more now than ever before. It's been two and a half years since the trial. And I feel like I'm only just coming out of it. I've stopped running from this dark thing. I'm standing and facing it.

Getting to this point, writing this, walking through this journey has built a resilience in me that I could never have imagined, I stand with boldness, and I stand in my power. It has taken me five years to reach this point in my recovery., It has never been easy but I'm here. I have had a few good people in my life that I trust who have walked with me, some part way and a few all the way. I am grateful to those who have stood with me regardless of the pressure.

Now, to you, my darling readers who are thinking of making a disclosure to the police, be prepared to lose people. It is inevitable. Be prepared to stand alone at times, there will be people who won't be able to handle it and remember its only people who are close to you who can hurt you. You will be okay. Every person you lose will be replaced by another. Be prepared for sleepless nights, be prepared for disappointment. Be prepared to release the residue of your past and be prepared to be stronger, wiser, bolder than you ever were before.

It is my opinion that the justice system is not designed for victims. I don't believe we will get the real justice we deserve, well, until the paedophiles in the judicial system are exposed or die. I did not get the verdict I wanted and if I'm honest I think I would still have the same opinion if he had been found guilty. However, I did get my day in court, I did get to speak my truth.

No-one can give me or anyone else back those years. It's been ripped out, taken, stolen, trampled on, pissed on. It was my choice to tell and it will be your choice and your choice alone if you decide to pursue it.

For me, it was the right thing to do, I am no longer a victim. The day I opened the door and walked into that police station was the day I decided my life was going to change, I decided never to let anyone silence me again. I decided to take authority over my own life, I decided to rescue my future, I decided to give myself a chance to live in freedom, with no shame and no self-blame.

I don't regret reporting it, as hard as it was, it was the beginning of my journey of letting go and forgiving myself. I've let go of the old and I am now rebuilding something breath-taking and new for my future.

Let me be clear, going to court doesn't take away the pain. It doesn't take away the hurt: in fact, it makes you confront yourself, as well as the perpetrator, and face your fears.

I needed to reconnect with myself, I wanted to discover who Yvonne Michèle really is, I needed to find my voice and own my power and this journey has helped me to do that. It has also helped me to help others find their voice and regain their power too.

I will never let what happened to me, destroy me, I will never allow him or what he did to me, to destroy me. I will not allow him or the court system to silence me, I will speak, I will live in my power and live in my truth.

You cannot change your past, but you can leave it behind and walk forward and embrace a breath-taking future with your head held high. Live in your truth. Face your demons, conquer your fears and live in your NOW.

We all have responsibility to tell our stories, by doing so we empower others to regain their life back too.

"We are the Voice of Freedom, together let us become the echo that brings down the walls for silence, shame and separation. Together we are strong, together we are one voice that will rebuilds, restructures and redefine our very existence!" Yvonne Michele

JUSTICE IS NOT RECOVERY
BY KATE, LONDON

I was twenty-six and living in London when the attack happened, nearly five years ago at the time of writing this.

I had met my future rapist on a bus on my way to work; he had handed me a flyer for the boxing gym where he worked. I had wanted to box for a while so two days later I was alone with him at the gym where he gave me a one on one training session, invited me for a drink afterwards and then raped me at his flat.

Reporting didn't even cross my mind for a number of reasons; I was scared of the repercussions from my attacker and staff where he worked, worried about not being taken seriously, I didn't want to cause a fuss and was still in shock and confused about what had happened. I didn't know he had committed a crime due to the circumstances and the fact I had been drunk, but I knew I had definitely been taken advantage of.

I decided to put it down to an unpleasant experience, brush it off and get on with my life. I even decided to go back to the boxing gym to carry on with training sessions, albeit with a different trainer because I didn't want what had happened to stop me from boxing and it was conveniently near to where I lived.

This meant I saw my attacker on a few occasions and each

time I did, he tried to force himself on to me when no-one was looking. Eventually after a couple of months I stopped going to the gym.

Then two years later I received a phone call from the manager of the gym who had accidentally called me thinking I was someone else. After the initial confusion we got chatting and I heard myself asking him if my attacker still worked there. His reply was "No, he's in prison for rape".

When I heard those words, I felt as if I'd left my body for a split second and immediately hurled the phone across the room before breaking down in tears. When I retrieved the phone from my bedroom floor I managed to blub down the receiver "he raped me too".

That moment was so surreal and yet my reaction so overwhelming and powerful that it scared me to realise how deep the wound was that I didn't even know was there. It was the first time I had cried or felt any emotion over what had happened.

From that point I knew I had to report, for my own dignity and self-worth, but more importantly for my sanity. I knew I had been slowly unravelling in the two years since I was attacked.

I felt safe knowing he was already in prison and thought that I was more likely to be believed as he was obviously already a convicted rapist. Knowing that other women had reported him also gave me courage.

I went with a friend to a police station and told the police woman through the glass partition at the front desk that I wanted to report a rape. She asked me to tell her what had happened in detail, so I stood there in the open and told her my story through the glass. She listened sympathetically but said as I didn't know his surname, or the exact location and date of the attack, I'd need to work out these details and come back.

I went home and became my own detective; I ordered my

past paper phone bills from my mobile phone company from that month two years ago and scoured them for my ex-boyfriend's number.

I knew I had called him immediately after, I also knew the time of day that I had called him and that we had spoken for about twenty minutes, we hadn't been in touch for a while, so I knew I would find that call. Once I had the exact date, I phoned the manager of the gym to ask for his surname and went back to the scene of the attack with my ex-boyfriend, wandering the neighbourhood trying to find the street and flat where he had taken me.

Before I had gathered all of my facts together a strange thing happened; On my way to work one morning I saw my attacker on the street. As I carried on walking toward him I felt nothing and apart from registering it was him I didn't even blink.

He grimaced at me in wry amusement, but I looked through him and walked on. He shouted after me "Oh, so it's like that is it?!"

When I got to work I was shaking and confused—I thought he was supposed to be in prison! Could he have just been let out? Was he ever in prison? Had the gym manager got it wrong?

I didn't even question not going ahead with reporting it even though it was obvious he wasn't in prison after all. It almost made me more determined after seeing him and knowing he was free to attack someone else.

Once I'd got all my information I went to a different police station closer to where I lived, and I was dealt with much better. There I was taken into a private room where I told my story to a police woman. I will never forget what she said once I'd finished; "This will probably be the hardest thing you'll ever have to do in your life, but you'll feel amazing when it's over".

I was told to expect a call in the next few days but when I went home later, the police had already been to my house and had left a note for me saying to call them urgently. It turned out they wanted me to come straight in and do my video statement in the morning. I had a feeling they knew exactly who my rapist was and how dangerous he could be.

The next day I went with a friend to the main police station who were in charge of sex offences, and after an initial panic attack and tears en-route in the taxi, I was led into a small room with two officers, one male one female, and calmly and honestly told them everything they asked me. Because it was a historic attack they told me not to worry if I couldn't remember everything and to just say "I can't remember" rather than try to guess any answers.

It took about an hour and a half and I surprised myself with small details I hadn't remembered until I was asked. There were some questions I didn't know the answer to like what the colour of his bedroom walls were or where the furniture was positioned. Some questions were difficult and seemed irrelevant to me, but the police explained this was future-proofing in case the defence later brought them up in court to use against me.

Once I was done, the police told me they were going to arrest him and gave me a panic phone to use in case I saw him again and he threatened or attacked me. It would call the police just by pressing a button, even if the phone was in my pocket. They weren't able to discuss any of his previous convictions with me or say if there were other victims, all they could tell me was that they were treating this case as mine solely. Not what I originally thought I was getting myself into but there was no going back now, and I was beginning to feel empowered although terrified at the same time.

A few weeks went by and they were still trying to locate him in order to arrest him, during which time every bus I got onto I thought I saw him. If someone was the same build, or skin tone or had the same hair cut as him I'd have a flash of panic before realising it was somebody else. Finally, they found him and arrested him, and he was remanded in custody overnight to appear in court the next morning to face charges. The CPS decided to press charges as there was enough evidence to present in court (his past offences, my phone bill statements and a poem I had written and emailed to a friend a month after it happened). They decided to release him on bail while awaiting trial.

I was told it could take a few months for the court date, but it ended up taking a whole year.

There was a mix up with the dates as it drew nearer; I had been told the trial would start on 2nd February but during a meeting with a police officer on New Year's Eve I discovered I'd been given the wrong date. It was actually scheduled for the 12th January, three weeks earlier than I thought. This may seem like a minor thing, but it was hugely anxiety provoking that suddenly I was going to go to court in less than two weeks, rather than in over a month's time as I'd been preparing for.

The police didn't apologise for the misinformation but in hindsight I'm glad it was sooner than I expected as there was less time to get worked up about appearing in court.

Because of the mix up with the dates I didn't have time for a pre-trial visit and the ISVA I'd been assigned to through the police and Victim Support wasn't exactly supportive. In fact, she had told me that I was probably going to get "ripped apart" by the defence. I couldn't believe she said that!

During the time I was waiting for the trial I was advised by Victim Support to not have any counselling until afterwards, as my therapy notes would be made available to the defence to potentially use against me. I personally feel that making a witness's past therapy notes available to the defence to scrutinise and twist is unfair and intruding. I've had other forms of therapy in the past for treating depression and all of those notes were shown to the defence. (In court they picked certain things out and questioned me about them even though the therapy notes were years old. One thing they picked on was my past difficulties in relationships with men and another was the fact I'd had depression in the past. To me these points were so irrelevant to what had taken place concerning my attacker that it made me both angry and amused. Luckily, I kept my cool and answered directly and with an air of "yes... and so what?". I like to think I made the defence lawyer look stupid and I think the jury could see through these weak attempts to discredit my character.)

Also during the year awaiting trial I was lucky enough to have some amazing support from a few close friends. I would talk to them about my worries surrounding going to court, going over details and anticipating possible questions from the defence. My biggest fear was standing up there and my mind going blank, or breaking down in tears or having a panic attack.

I did a lot of preparation, getting everything clear in my head about what had happened, making sure I was confronting every seed of doubt I had in my mind and doing lots of research into consent and other women's experiences of rape.

New government guidelines for juries around consent had just been introduced at the time and the message was that the absence of 'No' does not mean 'Yes'.

I found confidence in myself and became sure that what had happened to me was definitely rape, as yes, my mind was still throwing doubts at me even in the run up to the trial. It turns out this is very common, especially when drugs/alcohol are involved, or circumstances are different to the stereotypical 'stranger in a dark alley' rape scenario that society and the media has us believe is what constitutes rape.

I went through all of the natural emotions and uncertainties a lot of survivors have but often feel too ashamed or embarrassed to admit.

In court I was surprisingly less anxious than I expected I'd be and part of that was the spectacle of seeing the judge and barristers in wigs which made the whole thing seem like a bit of a pantomime. I had requested a screen in the courtroom, so I didn't have to see my attacker. Some people chose to look at them dead in the eye, but I wasn't that brave; I didn't want to be put off from delivering my evidence as confidently as I could.

I read my poem, submitted as evidence, to the courtroom which was a surreal but powerful experience. My ex-boyfriend also took the stand as a prosecution witness which is something I'll be eternally grateful to him for.

On the last day of the trial the jury took two hours to deliberate before returning a guilty verdict on two charges— one of rape and one of breaching a Sexual Offences Prevention Order (SOPO). When the police officer phoned me to tell me the verdict I reacted with a strange mix of joy and relief.

Ten weeks later he was sentenced to twelve years, serving a minimum of eight behind bars and ordered to sign the sex offenders register for life. There is an injunction against him for when he is released, stopping him from coming within a two-mile radius of where I live, although this will run out after a time.

I realise what an incredibly positive outcome I was fortunate enough to have had and I can't imagine going through all of that to have him found not guilty. It's a raw and vulnerable ordeal to go though, especially after having been raped in the first place.

It's now five years since the attack, three since I reported it and two since the trial, and yet I'm still in the process of recovery. It's been a very bumpy road to say the least but there have been some positive experiences that have come out of it. Six months before the trial I shaved all my hair off in aid of the

Massika fund, a refuge in the Democratic Republic of Congo for rape survivors and their children, and I managed to raise over £700. Rape is so common there and women are often disowned by their families once it's happened to them. It made me realise how lucky I am to live in a country with a justice system, freedom of speech and support networks available to me. I've also met some incredibly brave and inspiring women along the way.

In the future I hope to do something more active with my survival story but for now I'm taking my time to heal, day by day.

This is the poem I read out in court:

I was raped, wait, I know this is uncomfortable to hear
But you weren't there, you didn't feel that fear
Or see that face with that grin and those eyes that said
"You ain't going back to your place
You're stayin' right here, in this flat with me
And you're going to let me fuck you"
Well 'fuck you' I thought and so I fought,
And slapped him in the cheek
But he turned nasty and made me feel meek
I started to cry, begging the man who was about to rape me
for forgiveness
Told him I was sorry, it wasn't me
It must have been the weed that he had given me
I don't usually do this, I respect you. I respect you
I asked to go a million times and though yet no crime, I felt
uneasy
I didn't know that his mind had said no long ago
When I first agreed to go to his flat,
And he had envisioned us having sex
Not making love
This man was incapable of any meaningful intimacy

He only had to turn on his TV for me to see the kind of guy
he was
The channel set to porn
And then he confessed that he pays for virtual sex
To see them undress and caress their own bodies
And I started to realise this man is not right,
He's deprived, out of sight of real love and respect
I suspect he has issues with his own self confidence and worth
But what makes it worse is that he can't see,
The damage he's about to do to me
He hold the keys, literally
I'm locked in his yard
Nowhere to turn so he pushes me on the bed
My head spins and my body feels heavy
I know what's about to happen to me
So instead of fighting I'm resigning
I know what he wants and he's going to make sure he gets it
He's already erected so I close my eyes and try to enjoy it
And my mind blanks out the rest in self defence
It doesn't want me to know the devastating blow it received
that night
So it shuts it out tight
Fighting the memory of him violating me
But it doesn't end here
I'll remember next year and the year after that
The man who stole my spirit
Hijacked my femininity for one night of awkward sex
So he could get his pussy fix
And on to the next one, and on to the next

A DARK CHAPTER: RAPED IN A PARK BY A 15-YEAR OLD BOY

BY WINNIE M LI

I was twenty-nine when I was violently assaulted and raped in a West Belfast park by a complete stranger, a fifteen-year-old boy. It was a beautiful Saturday afternoon in the early spring, and I had intended to set off on an eleven-mile hike on my own, extending into the hills around Belfast, at the tail end of a business trip there. Ten minutes into my walk, I was approached by a strange boy, who said he was lost and needed directions. After a strained conversation with him, I continued on my way, eager to continue my solo hike, unaware he was still following me.

Further along the trail, he approached me again. This time he was not so friendly.

The rape that followed sparked a painful episode in my life, which years later inspired me to write my novel *Dark Chapter*. It's a fictional account of an assault similar to my real-life one, yet equally told from the perspectives of victim and perpetrator.

But that spring afternoon, moments after the assault ended, I had no idea that I might one day write a 382-page novel inspired by that incident. As 'newly-inducted' rape victims, we don't have that kind of foreknowledge, or even that sense of a possible future.

All we are thinking of is survival in the moment.

So after my teenage rapist had left the scene, I was thinking of survival, and I found myself covered in mud, shocked, sitting by the side of a trail in an unfamiliar forest, in the unfamiliar outskirts of Belfast. I didn't even really know where I was, as my hiking guidebook didn't have a detailed map. The main thought running through my mind was: did that really just happen?

And then: *how* could that have happened?

I had planned to go on an invigorating hike, and instead... instead... this weird thing had happened with a strange kid.

(I didn't use the word 'rape' at that moment, when I was still trying to make sense of things to myself). Briefly I considered continuing my hike, escaping from it all, clearing my head. But part of me knew I needed medical attention. I'd been punched, choked, forced to have unprotected sex with a complete stranger.... This was not one of those situations I knew how to handle on my own.

That was nine years ago, but I can still remember very clearly, the surreality of sitting by the trail debating what to do next: do I continue on my hike? Or do I call someone for help?

In some ways, that encapsulates the conundrum of the rape victim in the years after your trauma: do you attempt to go it alone, or do you ask for help?

That day, I asked for help. I made a definite turn away from the trail, walked to where I could hear a road with traffic, and as I walked, I phoned a friend.

It was a bizarre phone call, and one which I'd never imagined having to make. I still remember saying: "I'm not doing too well.... I think—I think I've just been raped".

That was the first time I used the word to describe my experience, almost out of necessity to get the help I needed.

'Rape' is a powerful word, a truthful word. We shouldn't be afraid to use it.

My friend called the police—and that set into motion a whole process of criminal justice which it never occurred to me to halt.

The police found me by the side of the road, after I gave them garbled directions. They asked for my account of the assault, walked me back to the crime scene, where I could point out what had happened where, and they set about collecting evidence. The whole time, I was thinking: is this actually *happening* to me?

In the meantime, I was taken in a police car to the Garnerville Care Suite in Belfast, subjected to hours of police interviews and then... the forensic exams.

For those of you who want further detail on the forensics, read my novel. I will conveniently skip over all that probing and swabbing to two days after my assault. Monday afternoon and I'm in my flatshare in London. All alone, as my flatmates are at work. They know about the assault, I've told them. I've even told my boss (who I work very closely with) and an immediate circle of friends, texting them: 'Just so you know, I was assaulted and raped on Saturday, so please don't ask how my weekend in Belfast went'.

In telling them that directly, I somehow wanted to hit the nail on the head, provide a straightforward explanation as to why I was acting so differently, how my life had changed so drastically in the course of an afternoon. I was lucky: none of my friends doubted me. Let's be honest, it's hard to imagine *why* a twenty-nine-year-old woman would ever make up a story about being violently raped in a park by a teenage stranger. I know it's different for other victims of other types of rape, and I can't imagine what it's like to be disbelieved, to have your own truth undermined and mocked. In all the years since, I've realised how 'lucky' I am that my rape fit the classic stranger rape scenario, and that I generally have a forthright personality.

But two days after the assault, I'm still in a huge state of shock, and I'm definitely not feeling lucky. I'm in front of my laptop and because I'm a naturally curious person, I type into Google: 'rape West Belfast' and hit search. I'm not expecting the stream of news reports which follows. Suddenly, I'm listening to a radio chat show about a 'wee Chinese girl' (me) who's been beaten and raped, presenters discussing what 'this horrific attack' means about the safety of Belfast. And while listening to complete strangers talk about my rape, I'm thinking: Where is there any space for *my* voice? The victim's voice? I'm a living person, too, you know.

Perhaps that experience prompted me many years later to start the work I now do as an activist and an author on the issue: because victims have a voice that deserves to be heard. Because survivors deserve to be respected and seen as individuals, capable of agency and recovery.

I was cast adrift for months after the assault, too traumatised to work or socialise, finding that the life I'd lived before my rape no longer fit post-traumatic Winnie. I felt like a ghost of my previous self, haunting the world of the living. The one thing I had linking me to anything concrete was this sense of a criminal justice process grinding onwards inevitably.

Following the media outcry over my rape, my perpetrator was eventually arrested five days later (rumour has it, he was compelled to turn himself in by his father. I'll never know the truth of this, but I've written that into my novel). He pleaded not guilty, and he continued to throughout the next eleven months.

Meanwhile, those eleven months were a miserable hell for me, because I knew at some point I would have to fly back to

Belfast to testify in court, in front of my own rapist about the details of my assault. My anxiety and PTSD rendered me unable to work, so all I could think about was the trial. Much of my distress came from the fact no one was explaining anything about the legal process at all to me. The police detective in Belfast reassured me the prosecution barristers would get in touch when appropriate, but the first time I heard from them was two weeks before the trial, over a video conference in the New Scotland Yard. The barristers mentioned there were special measures—if I wanted, I could testify behind a screen or via video link, so I didn't have to face my perpetrator, but they advised against it. 'I think they want you to break down in court,' my friend suggested. Because of course, the tearful rape victim would be the most convincing rape victim.

I didn't feel like I had any choice in the matter, so I just went ahead with the whole mystifying process, following their instructions, as I had been since that very first day when I phoned for help. Since my very first steps on that hike, I had entered unknown territory.

In March 2009, two close friends accompanied me back to Belfast for the trial. On the morning of the first day, when I sat as a nervous wreck at the courthouse, close to vomiting from the nausea, there was an expected turn of events: my perpetrator suddenly switched his plea to guilty. That was it: there would be no trial. I was free of having to testify. I had justice, yet it felt strangely anticlimactic. My friends were overjoyed; I was more in shock that the thing I'd dreaded the most was suddenly no longer going to happen.

'He must have been banking on the fact that you weren't going to show up to the trial,' someone explained. 'A lot of victims don't.'

In all those eleven months, it had never occurred to me to

back out of the legal process. I suppose I had a grim single-mindedness about it. An injustice had been done to me. I wanted that injustice to be recognised and answered for.

Six weeks later, I flew back to Belfast to attend the sentencing hearing of my rapist. I didn't have to, but part of me felt like I wanted to see this thing through to the very end. I sat a few seats away from my rapist's father, and listened as his son was sentenced to eight years in prison (half of his lifetime). In the end, because of a 50% remission policy in Northern Ireland, he only served four.

People often ask me if that's fair, but what is fair in this world? In the US, rape convictions carry much higher sentences. At the same time, many other rapes in this world are never even convicted. Was my own life immediately recovered and back to normal after four years? Of course not. But I'm not going to pin my own ability to recover on the mechanisms of a largely arbitrary, often flawed justice system.

At the same time, I'd be lying if I said the legal conviction didn't help with my recovery. Because I was lucky enough to get a conviction, I was able to draw a line under my own participation in the criminal justice process and tell myself: 'Hey, I did my best. He's been sentenced. Now I can focus on rebuilding my own life.' And because my crime took place in Northern Ireland, I was able to access that nation's Victims Compensation Scheme, which awards much higher tariffs than in England. It took over three years before I finally received those funds, but at least they cushioned the loss of earnings I suffered when I was unemployed for years after the assault. (PTSD and anxiety made it impossible to work in my demanding job as a film producer, and I eventually had to leave the country to find a job again.)

So all in all, I know I'm one of those rare cases, where I actually got a conviction. But the rape has still left an indelible impact on my life—on my career, my finances, my relationships, my chances of motherhood, my self-confidence, my very being. Every day since my assault, I've had to work towards restoring my sense of self. For a long time, I didn't think I'd ever be able to restore it.

Even before I started writing my novel in 2013, I knew I was going to write a trial scene, a fictional version of the court case that never happened in real life. Maybe the film producer in me knew that that's what audiences expect from having seen too many TV shows and movies: a Hollywood showdown in court, where the forces of justice win out. In researching my novel, I shadowed a barrister and sat through rape trials in London and Belfast. I was quickly horrified by what I saw: by the seemingly bored bureaucracy that dominates court rooms, by the lack of care given to victims on the day of their testimony, by the fact that these practically life-or-death outcomes were being handled by legal professionals who came from such privileged worlds, entirely different from the background of the people they represented. But mostly, I was shocked by the inhumanity of the cross-examination process. Victims were challenged, mocked, reduced to tears by defence barristers and this was how justice was meant to be achieved. I imagined how it would have felt to sit there on the stand, telling every single humiliating detail about being raped by a fifteen-year-old to a roomful of strangers—and then, to have that awful truth turned on its head, to have a barrister imply that I wanted it, I had agreed to consensual sex with my rapist. *That* kind of degradation is what constitutes our justice system.

So I wrote that into my novel. Most readers tell me that the courtroom scene is the most harrowing part of *Dark Chapter*, and that is its intended effect. I *want* people to get enraged. I *want* people to understanding how utterly unfair it is to have someone barge into your life and do this to you, and on top of that, to have our own government subject you to this kind of misery in the name of justice. And then, to add insult to injury, for there to be so few convictions. In all the court cases I witnessed, the defendants were acquitted. So all the cumulative years of stress and uncertainty those victims had to suffer, all the money spent on hiring barristers and transporting witnesses, all the police resources that went into the investigation—all that was for naught because the (alleged) perpetrators walked free in the end. What then, is the point of even having a criminal justice system?

I don't want to end this chapter on an angry note. There will always be anger, just like there will always be sadness when I think about my rape. There are years of my life that I will never regain—years when I could have been forging ahead in my career, making money, meeting new people and falling in love, enjoying the world. Instead, I was living like a ghost, in anxiety and fear. It took me years before I could regain the personality, the confidence, the drive that I had before the assault.

But I've managed to regain it, and along the way, I've learned that there is an incredible community out there of survivors and supporters who know what it's like, who understand the truth, and who increasingly, aren't afraid to address that truth. I dream of a day when we can all talk openly about our rape without feeling shame, without being judged. I dream of a day when our public institutions can serve the needs of victims and can properly assign guilt and accountability upon those deserve it. I'm willing to believe that day is coming. And I think we can all play a part in making it happen.

ABOUT WINNIE

Winnie M Li is an author and activist around the issue of sexual assault. Her debut novel, *Dark Chapter*, was published worldwide in 2017 and will be translated into nine languages. Partly inspired by her own stranger rape by a fifteen-year-old boy, it explores a rape from the perspective of both victim and perpetrator. The book won The Guardian's *Not The Booker Prize*, and was listed by Stylist Magazine as one of '10 Smashing Debut Novels of 2017.'

Her short-form essays and articles on the topic have appeared in The Times, The Mail on Sunday, The Independent, The Huffington Post, TIME, and elsewhere. She has been interviewed by outlets including The Guardian, BBC World News, Channel 4, The Irish Times, and is one of four survivors, who form the subject of the two-part TV documentary, Unbreakable: True Lives, which aired on TV3 Ireland in 2017.

Winnie is also the Co-Founder of the Clear Lines Festival, the UK's first-ever festival addressing sexual assault and consent through the arts and discussion. In London, she is part of the Angles project, dedicated to improving media coverage of sexual violence and domestic abuse. She is also a PhD researcher at the London School of Economics, researching the uses of social media by rape survivors to share their experiences and form a community.

Find more at:
- http://winniemli.com
- http://clearlines.org.uk/
- http://www.legendtimesgroup.co.uk/legend-press/books/1350-dark-chapter
- https://twitter.com/winniemli

PROFESSIONAL PERSPECTIVES

THE JUROR
INTERVIEW BY EMILY JACOB

I interviewed Fiona about her experience as a juror for a regional Crown Court in the autumn of 2016. This is my summary of that conversation, which Fiona has provided feedback and comment on, and which she has confirmed is an accurate reflection of her thoughts and feelings of that experience.

Fiona shared with me that she was excited to be given an opportunity to do her civic duty after receiving the jury summons, and went into it positively.

The first week she wasn't asked to sit on any cases. The second week, she was required to sit as a juror, and she talked about her unease that her excitement to be breaking the monotony of the previous week, was also going to be someone else's worst day.

It was an anal rape case within a relationship. Her heart sank.

The case was presented over two days, the jury then spent a day considering their judgement, and judgement was given at the end of the third day.

The victim, the woman, reported the anal rape a month after it had occurred, after the relationship had broken down. The defendant's barrister used the 'spurned woman' defence. However, the statement that her previous partner had provided for the court, and her testimony, were also powerful to hear.

She testified first and was on the stand for about two, to two and a half, hours. Fiona observed that the defendant's barrister didn't appear to be very good at his job; he didn't drill down in depth on the points, and when he did, he lost the jury. He was dismissive and patronising—and a thoroughly unlikeable man; distasteful.

The jury was representative in age and background. The racial split was minimal but reflective of the area being very white. There were four men. There was one mixed race. The youngest was a university student, the eldest a long-time retired teacher. There were a mix of professions and a spread of political views from communist to right wing.

Every juror took it seriously and committed to being fair. None of the women declared that they'd had experience of rape but there was the suggestion that some had experience of violence. Even so, none of the jury instantly jumped to belief, they all were committed to turning the evidence over and over.

There was no forensic evidence, the majority of the evidence presented was copies of social media messages. Some had been deleted, some retrieved. There were apologies from him to her. There were acknowledgements from her that she was not okay. There was not any explicit reference to what he was apologising for, or what she was not okay about.

The jury felt that he wasn't putting up a robust defence; he'd been injured after the incident and didn't have a full recollection and so couldn't answer a lot of the questions. The jurors felt that they had to interrogate everything on his behalf and be absolutely certain that the allegations had substance. Fiona mentioned that she had a personal friend who had been on the receiving end of a false allegation, and this was a factor in ensuring the defence got the best quality of treatment from the jury as possible.

The defence barrister suggested she was lying to get attention. He asked her about her previous sexual experiences, that she had an 'active' sex life. To which she replied, "what's wrong with that?" There was a discussion about whether she had consented to anal in the past; both acknowledged that nine to ten months earlier she had pushed him off when he'd tried previously.

Fiona commented that it was not easy to paint her in a negative light. She was a young mother; her ex-partner was supporting. She wore demure clothing, she was smart and neat. There was nothing in the case that saw the jury have to get over their preconceptions; she didn't come across as someone not credible. Fiona recognised that might well have been orchestrated but they had to weigh up who of the two was more likely to be credible, and there were holes in his evidence.

The first two hours of deliberation day were spent reviewing the details of the notes and the booklet of evidence that they were given.

No one juror led; it was very much a collaboration with two or three sharing the facilitation and making sure everyone was heard.

They had two questions that the judge had set them. Did anal sex occur, and was there consent?

There was general consensus that anal had occurred as he'd mostly acknowledged it on social media. Early on, there were about eight of the jurors whose instinct was enough for guilt. However, as a jury they wanted to go beyond instinct and be certain. Two of the women particularly felt instinctively he was guilty, but didn't feel there was enough evidence.

The end verdict was guilty.

Fiona doesn't know the sentence. The judge wanted medical reports on the injury the defendant had suffered since. She didn't want to find out the sentence afterwards; feeling that whatever it was, it would have been both too long, and too short. She was content to have done her bit.

Fiona commented that if this had been an allegation of vaginal rape and not anal rape, it might have been different. The victim was visibly distressed by the use of the word anal (excruciatingly uncomfortable). She also commented that it was the social media posts which helped provide the evidence the jury needed and that without them it would have been far more difficult to reach a verdict.

The victim was given 'special measures' in the courtroom and gave her evidence from behind a curtain shielding her from the accused. However, she had to walk in, and stare at the jury. And they had been instructed that they couldn't be warm, they needed to appear neutral. Fiona didn't know what support the victim would have had available to her, and hopes that counselling was offered. The woman was clearly suffering.

VICTIM BLAMING IS AT THE CORE OF THE CJS: JESSICA EATON

INTERVIEW BY EMILY JACOB

Jessica has spent eight years working in sexual violence. She started working in the courts, supporting victims through their trial, and then developed and managed the Vulnerable and Intimidated Witness (VIW) programme for the Midlands. In this role, she was responsible for two Crown Courts, and five Magistrates Courts. All the trials with VIWs were her responsibility, which could sometimes be up to twenty per day. Later on, she took on the role as Training and Service Manager of a rape centre which had over thirty psychotherapists and counsellors who specialised in helping anyone over the age of thirteen years old.

Before becoming independent in 2017, she was the Training and Research Manager in child sexual exploitation (CSE) and human trafficking. Within that role, she designed, accredited and delivered training to thousands of local authorities, mental health services, care homes and police forces each year.

Jessica is coming to the end of a PhD in Forensic Psychology and is a national specialist in victim blaming and victim psychology. She is now self-employed, undertaking forensic psychological research commissioned by universities, prisons, police forces, charities and local authorities. Jessica is an established public speaker and was shortlisted for the Emma Humphreys Award 2017. Her CV is remarkable, and I was honoured to speak with her.

Jessica opened our conversation by stating that the problem with this field is that some of the answers and solutions to the problems facing victims in the criminal justice system are already written into legislation. The Witness and Victim Charter is simply not followed in most cases, with victims and witnesses denied the most basic of rights. All those rights and protections are already there. Jessica stated that those rights and legislation can be ignored or not used adequately because there is very little belief in victims, their traumas and their need for protection and support. Professionals along the process have to weigh up whether to invest in resources when they don't believe the victims. Whilst most would expect professionals to be 'objective'—actually achieving objectivity is impossible. When children and adults give their statements, all professionals are capable of making a snap judgement. Fewer than 15% of victims ever report their experiences to the police to begin with. Even when they do, the large majority are not even getting as far as the CPS charging recommendations, with many police forces being found to have assigned it 'no further action' on the assumption that the victim is not credible enough or the case would never go anywhere, and therefore not worth the investigative time and resource.

It's rare for a police officer to have any training in terms of evidence assessment, so they don't get to the point where they're using the legislation. Complainants are simply not getting past the gate keepers.

Emma Sleath and Ray Bull demonstrated in 2014 that the

more specialist a police officer is, the more they endorse rape stereotypes and rape myths that blame the victim. This makes sense when we think about biases and how they develop. When sexual offences specialist teams only take forward stereotypical cases, knowing they will be taken seriously because the victim has presented with injuries, DNA and witnesses (for example), the officers become biased towards those cases that they think will make it to prosecution. Over a period of years, the officer takes the stereotype as a 'real' rape—and questions accounts that do not fit that mould (for example, cases where the victim is in a relationship with the abuser, has no injuries and has not reported quickly). It's assumed that a specialist team will become a team of objective experts, but it rarely happens this way and humans are known to be irrational decision makers.

The biggest problem in the criminal justice system is victim blaming.

Every single part of the process is underpinned by victim blaming. Could they have done something else, why didn't they leave, why did they drink, why were they wearing that, why did they walk home, why did they go back, why didn't they report, why don't they have any injuries...? The list goes on and on.

The same level of questioning is not given to the defendant; it is not their job to prove they didn't do it, but to argue that the victim isn't credible or that the evidence does not prove beyond reasonable doubt—which in many cases of sexual violence, is very difficult. Years ago, rapists were able to simply say 'it wasn't me' in court. However, since the development of DNA testing and forensic examinations, now their defence is usually based on 'yes, we did have sex, but it wasn't rape'—which means many victims end up arguing about consent in court— and the entire trial becomes an argument of whether the consent was clearly given.

The defence team has significantly more resources and more time with their client. They build a case and a story, and could meet between ten and fifteen times. The victim could meet the CPS ten minutes before the trial starts, having never met a lawyer in their life. This results in a complete stranger taking them through their evidence in chief. Meanwhile, the defence gets the opportunity to discredit the victim with background information. Jessica asked, how is it fair that the defendant gets to rehearse and gets copies of video evidence, whilst the victim gets it ten minutes before? How is it fair that the defendant can be protected from the jury knowing anything about their past, so it does not 'bias the jury' but the victim can have their entire lives laid out, including their sex life, mental health records and so on? Victims attend court and they are told, 'read over this to remember what you said all that time ago'. It's instantly biased— some victims and witnesses have looked at Jessica and said, 'I don't remember saying any of this...'. Jessica adds here that we know from significant academic research that it's virtually impossible for a traumatised victim to remember their trauma in perfect, objective detail months or years later for a court case—so why would we further impact that process by leaving it so late for the victim to read their own statement?

An example Jessica gave from a case she worked on in 2013:

A sixteen-year-old girl had been battered to an inch of her life. She was headbutted twelve times in the face by a man in his twenties who had been raping and abusing her. She was given her statement on the morning of court: nine pages in doctors-like illegible handwriting by the police who'd taken her statement originally. Classified as a VIW, she needed much more preparation than that! The defence and the defendant had dreamt up an elaborate story, and she was just trying to remember the basics. They brought up her CAMHS records for self-harm and previous sectioning from when she was just eleven years old—they used her records to argue that the injuries were self-inflicted. No-one knew that was going to be admitted into evidence. Her jaw dropped. How was she supposed to respond to the accusation that she had caused all those injuries herself? She should have been entitled to special measures, to not appear in court at all, to have a screen, to have a live link. She should have had more breaks. The prosecutor should have advocated for her to have a break, the magistrate should have done their jobs.

The defence solicitors and defendants have become more intelligent with 'not guilty' pleas. Now, it's 'yes it happened, but not like that'. So, the trial deliberately becomes a war of words, one against the other. The defence are much better at discrediting people than the prosecution who just present the case in a lot of examples Jessica has seen. The defence rip the victims apart, they don't care. Jessica has seen them do it to seven-year-old children. In research about sexual abuse and sexual exploitation, children have told us that the trial was worse than the abuse. One report published in CSE actually cited a child saying that the cross examination was 'like being raped all over again'. We cannot stand by a system that creates that level of trauma in victims.

Jessica dealt with a case in 2012 where a seven-year-old was hit by a truck and experienced significant life changing injuries including two broken legs and internal injuries. The defence tried to say it was her fault for not looking properly near the road. Because she cried in the live link room, and her evidence could not be heard through her sobbing for her Mum and Dad, the charges were dropped. People say these things are impossible in modern day court, but it became an everyday occurrence for Jessica.

In 2013, Jessica dealt with another case of a woman in her twenties who was among a number of victims in her family who were raped by their Grandad, who was then in his seventies. Jessica watched as the defendant manipulated the entire trial. He started off by saying that he was deaf (which was believed without testing) and said that he couldn't hear the evidence well enough through the live link provided for the victims, so he needed them to come into court—otherwise the trial would not be fair. Hours later, he said that his hearing aid was playing up and he needed to sit closer to the victims and to take the screens down, so he could hear them give evidence properly— otherwise the trial would not be fair. Hours later, he said that he needed to be able to lip read the victims whilst they gave evidence and requested to sit next to them whilst they all gave evidence. Every single requested was granted in Jessica's court and despite Jessica arguing against each request. This resulted in a number of victims being completely traumatised, couldn't concentrate and the man was found not guilty.

We now have a system where the victim needs to one hundred per cent prove their case whilst the defence barrister's only job is simply about 'can they discredit the victim so that they are not taken seriously, and the jury can't reach a unanimous guilty verdict?'

As a result of these experiences and many more with the police and legal system, Jessica doesn't advise prosecution anymore. The damage and the trauma are immense, and there is so much evidence that the process induces PTSD and be much more likely to suffer trauma responses—that the benefits do not outweigh the impact. It's not just retraumatising to tell it again, but you're challenged on every level, over and over again.

The language in the system is very biased. It used to be that defence would suggest the victim was "attention seeking"—now it's seen a definite shift towards "compensation seeking"—and the major problem with this is that when defence barristers use tactics like this, it is enough to influence a jury of biased members of the public, many of which read the tabloids every day (who are known to be anti-victim). A general-public jury will fall for those tactics and will think that victims are going through this entire process for a few grand. It fits the national narrative of demonising victims.

The defence will say things like, "They went back to the abuser", and then deliberately ask does that sound like a victim, to you?

The whole system right from the beginning is about, is the victim credible? Are they the 'infallible victim'? Because if they are not, they are in for a hard time.

There are especially very low levels of those with learning disabilities getting past the police station. Jessica explained a case of a girl with autism, who was only fourteen years old. In five years, she's reported eleven rapes, all by different people but in the same kind of grooming style and offence. Every single one has been NFA'd (no further action) and the professionals working with her are being told she is not credible enough because of her autism.

Jessica founded The Eaton Foundation, a charity for male mental health (in 2013 it was the first male mental health centre in the UK). One of the clients, a male in his forties, but with a mental age of eight was raped a few weeks previously. The way the police dealt with it was appalling, including a police interview carried out in a safe and familiar environment that was not recorded properly, so they said they had to book him in to do it all over again.

When the client got to the police station, he became scared because he thought he was in trouble. The officer doing the interview admitted that he had no training in interviewing adults with profound learning needs and low mental ages and kept stopping the interview to go and find his sergeant to ask what to do. The sergeant told him to get on with his job and the officer admitted this to the staff member. The client was entitled to an intermediary and a highly trained officer, but this was not followed. Instead, the rapist (a known sex offender with multiple prison sentences) made a counter-allegation that the client raped him instead and at the time of writing, this was being taken forward because the other client could not defend himself as he didn't understand the allegations. The Eaton Foundation has worked hard in this case to protect the client from legal action and from the poor practice of the police force. The reality is, however, why was this needed? How can evidence collection be this poor in 2017?

In 1999, Payne et al. developed the IRMAS, Illinois Rape Myth Scale. IRMAS is a psychometric scale of how the general public accept or respond to rape myths. Over a long period of time it's been proven to have an extremely high validity and reliability over multiple population studies. An updated study by McMahon and Farmer (2010) was also developed, in which young people were consulted about the validity of the scale. The findings showed how victim blaming is becoming more subtle, palatable, and socially acceptable. Certain items that were used in 1999 were considered obsolete in 2010 because young people realised that victim blaming was not socially desirable.

However, Jessica argues that the language has simply shifted from 'to blame' to 'need to be responsible', and 'did the behaviour of the victim *cause* it to happen.' People will often say 'I'm not saying they are *to blame* for being raped, but they have to accept that if they were not walking down that road then it wouldn't have happened, and they are *responsible* for their own safety!' Jessica is currently writing a paper on this concept.

Victim blaming is undermining every stage of the justice system. When I asked her, Jessica said that if she had a magic wand, she would remove victim blaming and bias from the system.

Jessica has recently developed a new psychometric measure that tests implicit victim blaming in humans. She has a vision to use it to screen the police, CPS, and jurors on victim blaming, bias and rape myth acceptance. We already screen people for racism—why not victim blaming? She would use her scientifically valid measure to remove victim blaming from the process. I like this vision, and hope wholeheartedly that it will come true.

ABOUT JESSICA EATON

Jessica Eaton is a national academic researcher, writer and speaker in the forensic psychology of sexual violence, mental health and feminism. She has a career history in the development, management and training of rape centres, police forces, criminal justice system services, local authorities and therapeutic services. She specialises in the victim blaming of women and girls who have experienced sexual violence and abuse—and the societal structures that encourage and perpetuate victim blaming and self-blame after sexual violence. Jessica performs and writes psychological research, evaluations, delivers speeches, lectures and workshops and has appeared on many radio stations and TV channels discussing sexual violence and mental health.

- Website: www.victimfocus.org.uk
- Email: jessica@victimfocus.org.uk
- Twitter: @JessicaE13Eaton
- Facebook: www.facebook.com/jessicaforenpsych/

SPECIAL MEASURES FOR ALL: RHIANNON EVANS

INTERVIEW BY EMILY JACOB

Rhiannon is the Director of Services at *Supporting Justice*, and is an experienced practitioner in directly supporting victims and witnesses. It was an honour to speak to her about her work and her perspective of the Justice System.

Rhiannon opened by explaining that whilst sexual violence is often considered taboo within society, within the criminal justice world the cases take up a large portion of court time. It's a really common practice. However, it's a crime that feels far removed from many people's lives and as a result the taboo exists for the friends and family and others who aren't familiar with it.

A taboo is created by people not talking about things, and although we need to talk about sexual violence, one of the key issues preventing people talking is that there is so much in the criminal justice system that is confidential. This isolates victims and it creates a level of suspicion amongst both victims and friends and family. Those in the system tread on eggshells to make sure they're not oversharing, and anonymity can be isolating for the victim.

For the victim, reporting (or disclosure as it's called in the criminal justice world) is further complicated in terms of who might support you later down the line because of cross-contamination of evidence: the person you first disclose to is likely to be called as a witness, and once you've given a statement you shouldn't discuss the evidence.

Rhiannon supported someone recently, who had reported childhood sex abuse. When she reported it, she had someone with her to support her. That person was then later questioned on the stand about the level of information shared, with the inference that the person had been coached into giving their story.

If you're a victim you often share multiple times with people close to you, before you have the courage to report it to a professional agency. It's like you have to tell people you trust to work out if it's something you can share with the wider world: you need the confidence that it's possible. Rhiannon described a training exercise which she attributed to the Birmingham Rape and Sexual Violence Project which she now uses to help people imagine sexual violence disclosure: the exercise encourages people to share their best sexual experience in pairs. It's really uncomfortable for them. Of course, participants are stopped before they actually disclose but it helps them to imagine how it might feel to sharing your worst sexual experience. If you can't share your best, how do you find the words to share your worst?

However, Rhiannon observes, the process of victims sharing with others is risky for criminal justice agencies, as it's important that stories aren't rehearsed, and victims aren't being coached. Obviously, people can't be expected to hold everything in, so the criminal justice system needs to realise that it's going to happen.

Another issue is that when the victim gives the report, it needs to be evidential. Timelines are always important in establishing the facts in a trial. But in sexual assault, timelines are often difficult. Victims are asked multiple questions and as a result sometimes they are may think they gave the wrong answer. Actually, they haven't: it's just the interviewer is taking things in order and knows the point they are trying to establish. Unfortunately, victims can easily second-guess themselves. Rhiannon doesn't think that we explore enough with victims why a question may be asked, or set the expectation regarding what will happen in the questioning: e.g. starting from the beginning, repeating questions, and/or go over an event several times from different angles.

Rhiannon believes that training is still absolutely key to getting a good first interaction and putting a victim at ease. Victims need to feel they've been believed. The police and all other agencies need to be careful to treat each victim as an individual reporting for the first time. With so much sexual violence coming into court it would be easy to consider the victim as "just another one". This is important as the biggest need for victims is information, but when there is so much sexual violence in the system, it can be easy for agencies to assume a level of knowledge and forget to explain procedures and give out information. Victims don't automatically gain a great knowledge of the criminal justice system just by being unlucky enough to become a victim.

For victims, being questioned by police is an intense experience. And they might need to be questioned on multiple occasions. It would be better for victims to be asked what works for them, for the victim to be more involved in the planning, whether they want long sessions, or shorter sessions.

In order to improve outcomes in sexual violence reporting and justice, Rhiannon believes we need to go back to basics. The solution is training, and speaking and listening to victims. Police officers get an initial training course which lasts for many weeks; in the early part of this training they undergo a community placement. Rhiannon has experience of hosting these placements. She explained how they were extremely valuable as new police officers would get the chance to speak to real victims, something they have probably never done and may not do again for the whole of their training. There isn't enough direct interaction with real victim and that is often because they're worried about revictimizing victims.

The CPS and police are very anxious about pre-trial therapy, and often victims are told it's not permitted whilst a case is waiting for court. But it is absolutely the case that it is allowed. Yet, because people are worried about it, they sometimes don't offer it. It can also take a lot of effort to organise as it requires a specialist, and there aren't many people practising. Plus, there is red tape to ensure that the pre-trial therapy has been appropriately explained to the court. Rhiannon believe that it's these barriers that often puts people off offering it to victims.

It can also be something that the defence can interrogate in the same way they can question all the evidence. Yet it can be very detrimental to the victims who need it, if it's delayed. Ultimately it should be the victim's choice, but Rhiannon believes pre-trial therapy should at least be offered to everyone as a right.

Rhiannon explains that pre-trial therapy is made even more important as another issue is the wait-time for cases to come to court. Potentially victims wouldn't need pre-trial therapy if the case could get to court quicker. In the Crown Court you can wait a year for a trial, and in Magistrates six months, and there are often adjournments to the original trial date.

The implementation of the Section 28 special measure might have an impact on the wait time. Special measures include giving evidence behind a screen, going to a different court, or a different venue, removals of gowns and wigs. Special measures are only available to those who are classified as a Vulnerable or Intimidated Witness. (A Vulnerable and Intimidated Witness is a specific definition of witnesses but includes the categories of sexual violence, domestic violence, gang related violence, guns, or knife crime, as well as others). An existing special measure is pre-recorded video evidence which means the tape is played for the court. The new Section 28 addition is to also allow cross-examination to take place in advance on tape. It's been tested in three or four courts over the last couple of years, and is being rolled out nationally in September 2017, for children only initially and with the intention for all eventually. It would mean that victims wouldn't have to wait for the main trial to happen to receive therapy. However, friends and family will still have to wait for the trial to give evidence as they are unlikely to fall under the vulnerable and intimidated witness definition.

Waiting times are a problem because essentially victims have to rehearse in their heads their evidence while waiting for it to come to trial. Not all trials get fixed dates (if it's heard in Crown Court; Magistrates are fixed). If it's a vulnerable victim or witness, they try to, but not always. A period of two weeks is usually given, and the night before, they get a phone call. But, the fixed day isn't usually a fixed time. It could be 2pm instead of 10am, and go into the next day.

Rhiannon firmly believes that victims should get choice about what happens. Best practice dictates that, victims don't need to watch their video statement at the same time as the jury, they can watch it before. However, many victims don't get the choice, they're not presented with options, they're presented with the norm which is usually what is convenient for the system.

Victims are meant to get a choice over their special measures, it's supposed to be an informed choice. Most people are presented with the special measure they're going to have.

Old school thinking is that the optics and impression is better if victims appear in person rather than behind screens, and victims were in the past discouraged from taking up special measures. That time seems to have passed. Ultimately the victim should give their evidence in whatever form is best for them.

Victims are still discouraged from going back to courtroom, especially if they've taken advantage of special measures as the perception might be that they're not scared after all. But listening to evidence and being questioned in front of people are very different.

So what support is out there for witnesses? Rhiannon spoke about how the Citizens Advice Witness Service has a responsibility to prepare victims and witnesses for court when the defendant pleads not guilty. The Witness Care Unit, run by the police, will ask what the needs are for the witness. They are trying to establish, what the issues are that would prevent this witness going to court and giving evidence, so it includes understanding people's needs for special measures. As part of that they should offer the Witness Service to the victim or witness—but they can't always do this as Witness Care Units don't actually call all witnesses to make the offer, in which case the referral is more of a signpost through a letter. The person has to give the police their consent for their details to be passed on. Sometimes the question will be phrased "You don't need this do you?". If someone has an ISVA, the assumption is often that you don't need it. But the Witness Service know the courts inside and out, they know the judges. The ISVA is the crisis point, and support. The Witness Service are impartial, and so they're allowed to sit with the witness through special measures, the ISVAs often aren't allowed.

The Witness Service outreach service will go to the witness' home to talk about the process. Especially for children this can be really important, it's similar to the preparation you might do with your child to not be scared of the first day at school. A pre-trial visit to the court is also offered, or it can be done over the phone. Some people meet the Witness Service on the day. The guess is that the majority of witnesses receive the Witness Service support on the day, as they are asked to wait in the Witness Service manned waiting rooms based in the court house. The Witness Service is massively valuable. The gap is that the other agencies need to see the benefit of it.

So what could be improved? Rhiannon observed, if victims could be warned when needed via text, instead of sitting around, that would be an improvement. It's very isolating to have to sit in a separate room, it can feel like you're in custody.

The actual experience of giving evidence and talking about it in front of people is very intrusive. The court environment could be changed to be less formal. Rhiannon observes though that there is a balance between informality to ease anxiety, and the need for formality to represent the seriousness of the situation.

Rhiannon concluded by wishing that the whole system treated people as individuals with fewer barriers and potentially more people being able to access the special measures that are on offer to vulnerable people. And she absolutely wants there to be more training for everyone who comes into contact with victims. Criminal justice system agencies often try to protect victims, but sometimes this protection results in people choosing for victims rather than giving them their own choice. From a training perspective, the first encounter is particularly important, and, throughout the process, there are multiple first encounters so if we could get that right satisfaction would most definitely increase.

ABOUT RHIANNON EVANS

As Director of Services for *Supporting Justice*, a community interest company working to improve policy and services for victims and witnesses of crime, Rhiannon works with a whole range of different organisations. One of the largest part of her role is working alongside Citizens Advice, providing daily subject matter expertise to the senior management team. She has managed several projects including leading their service re-design and supporting the implementation of a new training programme and new digital services.

Previously, Rhiannon worked for thirteen years with the national charity Victim Support, latterly serving as Divisional Manager for the Avon and Somerset, Devon and Cornwall and Dorset police force areas. Having worked through the charity starting from the grassroots as volunteer directly supporting victims, predominantly of serious crime, she has overseen the design, development and implementation of new projects including services for domestic violence, anti-social behaviour and restorative justice.

Rhiannon has been the voice of victims and witnesses in many forums, at seminars, workshops and conferences across Europe. She also has played a crucial role in securing funding from various different funding streams. Other roles have included managing a team of Independent Domestic Violence Advocates (IDVAs), working as a caseworker within the Crown Prosecution Service, a mediator for high risk gangs and a restorative practice worker for Birmingham Youth Offending Team.

If you are a victim of crime and need support, find local service at www.victimschoice.org.uk

BIG SHIFTS ARE IN SIGHT:
DR SARAH HEKE
INTERVIEW BY EMILY JACOB

Sarah has worked with the Criminal Justice System for around thirteen years; she is currently chair of the independent advisory group to the Metropolitan Police, advising on rape, sexual assault, child sexual abuse and exploitation. She is a consultant clinical psychologist and has expertise in C-PTSD.

The Right Honourable Dame Elish Angiolini was commissioned in June 2014 by the Commissioner, Sir Bernard Hogan-Howe, and Director of Public Prosecutions, Alison Saunders to independently review all aspects of the Criminal Justice System, including the conviction rates and the experiences of victims. This was in response to the significant increase in reports of rape and sexual assault, including non-recent abuse following Operation Yewtree. It made forty-six recommendations, the implementation of which Sarah has been involved with working alongside senior CPS and the Metropolitan Police colleagues. This has been very much working collaboratively together.

Working more closely together is one of the biggest changes to be influenced by the Dame Elish Review: how the different departments across the police, CPS, health and voluntary sector services have started to make significant changes, especially in looking at for instance, how forensic evidence is used and streamlining some of the court processes and decision-making.

From a psychological point of view one of the key recommendations of the Review was in updating the CPS guidance for the provision of pre-trial therapy. The 2001 guidance had caused lots of difficulties due to misinterpretations from all involved—and Sarah has been working together with the voluntary sector, Rape Crisis, the CPS policy department and NHS England, to name a few bodies who are involved.

One of the key issues of that guidance had been that some people had been prevented from accessing therapy. There was a feeling that therapy could 'undermine the case' with therapists 'coaching' victims—which is unhelpful language. Now there is starting to be a shared understanding of what therapy involves and what is meant by therapeutic support, to avoid those with different professional backgrounds having different interpretations. Sarah is hopeful that this updated guidance will start to change practice and access to therapy will no longer be the decision of the police, or the CPS, or the therapist but the individual's.

When it comes to pre-trial therapy, there needs to be an understanding on the part of the therapist, and the victim, that some testimony may be relevant to the court when details of the assaults are discussed in detail as a necessary part of the therapy, for instance in processing traumatic memories. This needs client consent. But there also has to be clear understanding which elements are relevant to the court, and which are not. Victim history has been allowed for the defence case for some time, [Editor's note: don't get me started....] but in these changes, only relevant evidence would be permitted. Sarah explains that the new guidance is trying to move away from 'therapy as coaching'. She and the team are writing it right now, and the earliest it will be signed off and adopted could be Spring of 2018. [Editor's note: I'm watching that space hopefully; too many of my clients were denied pre-trial therapy when it was evidently required.]

Another change that's on its way is the ability to introduce psychological evidence into trials: the acknowledgment that memory loss, and mixed-up timelines is normal, and acceptance that sexual trauma has a psychological impact. Further Dame Elish recommended that psychological evidence regarding victim's responses, such as 'fight, flight and freeze' physiological responses, should be provided within the context of understanding the brain's response to traumatic events. Expert testimony on the psychological impact of sexual trauma was in the past considered inadmissible, however now the precedent is beginning to be set. Professors' Chris Brewin and Bernice Andrews, experts on PTSD and traumatic memory at UCL and Royal Holloway, have completed a thorough systematic review on the research evidence of false memory which had been a big sticking point in disclosure and other areas. They've dispelled a lot of myths and shown that whilst it is possible to create specific conditions for generating false memories, and they can exist, the conditions have to be very specific and even then, it only occurs in few people. Information on traumatic memory processing is being incorporated into the pre-trial therapy guidance too.

Sarah wants me to be clear in writing up this interview that these changes are being proposed, and are not yet agreed.

Sarah, along with her colleagues, is also working to challenge a lot of the media representations of rape and sexual assault. The general public support a lot of the rape myths because the media share them. A rape is still considered to primarily happen by a stranger in an alleyway. But generally, it is by the people you know, in a very different context to the alleyway. And the media is still responsible for blaming victims. False allegations are rare, yet the media will pick up on false allegations, and blame that person, without any understanding of how someone would get to that place.

At the end of the day, within the Criminal Justice System, it comes down to the jury. Judges can issue directions to the jury, although often they do not. It comes down to how the jury perceives the victim, and how the evidence is presented, and their own preconceptions. So, changing the CJS outcomes is very challenging. There are more public campaigns now, like the 'cup of tea', and the message that a victim doesn't have to say no, and often cannot. For many victims it is physiologically impossible to say no, when they are under psychological threat. The focus needs to shift from rape being the responsibility of victims to say no, to understanding the more complex dynamics at play. 'Freeze' is the most common response immediately during rape and sexual assault, and the general public need to understand that.

Another issue with the pursuit of justice for victims is that there is a lot of really good practice, but people don't often know about the many people doing this. Within all the professional agencies, the CPS, MPS, and NHS, people get moved around a lot, continuity is lost and so it's hard to foster relationships. Another recommendation by Dame Elish was to give more training on rape myths and stereotypes to the CPS and MPS, something Sarah and her psychology colleagues had also done ten years ago; she felt like she had come full circle. This is not to say that it not still valuable.

The Dame Elish Review has given direction to all the involved organisations. They have had to respond, which is what is so different than the past, because things are changing at the governmental level. For Sarah now, and listening to her, it feels like some major shifts in the right direction are about to happen, because the departments are working collaboratively to find the solutions.

Sarah acknowledges that there will still be some big questions. What is next? What impact will these changes have? How much time will they take to be adopted? Will they be adopted across the country? The Dame Elish Review was very specific to London and it needs to be taken to other areas. London has thousands of cases; what happens in a rural police force that sees few rapes reported? How can the learning be shared?

Sarah observes though that the changes are happening, and that the more cases go to court where people have had pre-trial therapy, and the psychological aspects can be admitted, rather than a reliance on DNA and he-said/she-said, the more the changes will continue to happen. It will take time. But for the number of people involved, it will be huge.

What these changes don't do is support those who have chosen not to report. For all victims, there is a psychological response; it's a very personal violation, self-blame is common. It's one of the few crimes that self-blame is a phenomenon; we don't blame ourselves when our car is broken into, or we're mugged on the street. Rape is a very internally personal experience, and making sense of what's happening is difficult. At least 50% may develop PTSD. Victims will be re-experiencing the trauma whilst trying to put their life together: the system hasn't supported this, or the wider impact on people's lives.

Therapists ask questions too; often they don't understand the Criminal Justice System either. How do we disseminate good practice so that everyone can make the right choices? It's so difficult to define primarily because it's such an individual experience. In the end, it must be about what the person gets in support alongside the CJS. And there is a massive gap in the support structure. There's a promise of therapy. But there's a huge variation in people's skills and knowledge, across the prosecution, the police, and therapy providers. Someone could be seeing a therapist for anxiety—and then suddenly disclose a rape and that therapist might never have handled that kind of disclosure before. A police officer might have always taken reports of burglaries or car crime, and suddenly is hearing the reports of a victim of rape. Yet it's so important when these professionals are disclosed to that they don't get it wrong. The questions they ask of the victim in the immediacy of that disclosure will either make the victim feel believed, or not.

Sarah's response when I asked her what one thing she would change if she had a magic wand and one wish was telling: she couldn't choose. There's not one thing that needs to change; there are so many different parts that need to change. She hopes that the shifts that are being proposed that will lead to a wider understanding of the psychological impacts of rape and sexual assault will be significant.

Sarah ended by musing on the facts that whilst we must acknowledge the significant psychological impact and how it affects people's lives in ways other traumatic events don't, and we can't underestimate that, some people do manage to do amazingly well. There is no need for victims to take on those labels, it is possible to cope and more forward and make positive changes as a consequence of the trauma. This chimed in with my own beliefs that we mustn't get lost in the victimhood of being victimised, that we can move on and move forward and re-create the life we want to live.

ABOUT DR SARAH HEKE

Sarah was Consultant Clinical Psychologist and Director of the Institute of Psychotrauma, the specialist complex and severe

Post Traumatic Stress Disorder service for East London Foundation NHS Trust for the past 8 years and has recently joined the new team at the Grenfell Health and Wellbeing Service. She was also previously Lead Clinical Psychologist at the Haven Whitechapel, the specialist forensic medical service for people affected by rape and sexual assault and the HIV and sexual health service at Barts and the Royal London NHS Trust. She has provided psychological therapy and specialist assessment to over one thousand women, men and young people including refugees and asylum seekers.

Sarah has provided training and lectured on sexual and domestic violence to health, medical, police and legal professionals on a national and international basis and has numerous other peer-reviewed publications in health-related journals.

Sarah has been very actively involved in promoting psychological evidence and understanding the psychological impact of rape, sexual assault and child sexual abuse in the Criminal Justice System. She is Chair of the Rape Reference Group for the Metropolitan Police Service, Secretary of the UK Psychological Trauma Society and Chair of the Royal College of Psychiatry Accreditation of Psychological Therapies Committee.

THE ISVA PERSPECTIVE
BY ANNIE ROSE & LYNNE TOOZE

Some people will want justice for the crime committed against them and they may seek this via and through the system they believe and understand will deliver—the Criminal Justice System (CJS). The purpose of the CJS is *'to deliver justice for all, by convicting and punishing the guilty and helping them to stop offending, while protecting the innocent.'* (www.cjsonline.gov.uk) and *'... to deliver an efficient, effective, accountable and fair justice process for the public.'* (*Working Together to Cut Crime and Deliver Justice*, 2007).

As ISVAs we support individuals who have experienced sexual violence and have reported, or are thinking about reporting, to the police. It's a tough decision and there is no advice which can be given to make that decision easier. An individual can be given all the information around the process they may enter into, but it will be an individual journey and there are no guarantees of success. It may be short if the investigation is NFA'd (no further action) and then closed, or it may be long if the case eventually goes to court. At no point will it change what has happened and for a few, there may be a sort of justice if the perpetrator is found guilty and sent to prison. The number of individuals who see the person who abused them go to prison is small. Even then, for many individuals, the fear will return when the perpetrator is released, such is the impact of sexual violence and the legacy of this type of abuse.

Sexual violence is traumatic and is viewed as a crime second only to homicide in its violence and gravity within the CJS. It is therefore strange and incomprehensible that so many excuses for, and myths around, rape and sexual assault are so readily found in our society. Society recoils from accepting what rape really is, how traumatizing and damaging it is and how prevalent it is against women, young people and children. The responsibility is shifted to the victim all too frequently and assumptions, rape myths, and negation of seriousness seem to become normal responses and reactions.

Alcohol, drugs, sexual history, mental health, sexual preferences, sexuality, learning disability, disability culture, race and even immigration status become weapons to use against victims. It's an insidious and destructive force which seeks to undermine a victim's experience with all manner of irrelevancies. Many victims will report, many victims will not. There is no right or wrong response. The decision a person makes will be a difficult one either way

The Criminal Justice System is a process which has been developed to sit at the heart of justice, the law and criminal activity, with a purpose to make safer the society we live in.

There are issues which are specific to certain groups of people, but also issues which are universal when a person has experienced sexual assault and rape. For young people and adults with a learning disability, there is often a significant waiting period for an intermediary to become available to support the process of taking a statement from the victim. This is counter-productive as memory is often not as clear after time. There is a general rule that a statement should be taken as soon as possible. The wait is generally due to the lack of available intermediaries.

Added to this, the wait for a case to get to court is, more often than not, too long. When a case does go to court, the case should be heard by a specialist judge, trained to oversee rape cases.

However, it seems that there is not enough training for others involved in the CJS—including front line police officers and barristers within the CPS. There needs to be more training around rape myths, trauma and memory. There is also a need for judges and others involved in the CJS to receive training around learning disability and/or autism.

The decisions around taking a case to court need to be more transparent and the CPS needs to be more knowledgeable about trauma, rape myths and be able to bring in expert witnesses and/or make fair arguments to the jury around how trauma can affect a person.

If a case goes to court, there needs to be more information disseminated to the jury around myths in society concerning rape and sexual assault. There is a lack of understanding also around how traumatic sexual violence is and how the impact (psychological, physical, emotional) may affect the retelling and recall of the incident. A victim may present in the ABE (Achieving Best Evidence) video statement as emotional, or not, and be able to recall incidents, or not. They may even confuse items, places and times. When traumatised, memory is not necessarily linear or clear.

Juries need to have special instructions/training in consent, sexual violence and the reality of facing a perpetrator who is known to the victim: a partner, family member, work colleague, and/or friend/acquaintance. What is the reality in this situation—what is consent? How can consent be consent if the victim is too terrified to say no, is too drunk to be able to choose? These areas tend to bring up emotional responses from people and some very strange reactions. Blaming the victim seems to become easier: why did she meet up with a violent ex-partner? Why did she go for a drink with him? Why didn't she fight him off? There are also some very unreasonable assumptions about women, when sexual violence comes into an argument, and those assumptions are formed from gender-based violence.

For people with a learning disability, everything can be lessened as they are frequently deemed as less deserving, less worthy and/or should be grateful for any attention. They may not react in ways which others would believe to be appropriate i.e. smiling when they are in fact terrified.

There needs also to be more understanding of how victims will react when involved with the police; more training around assumption, meaning and judgments. There should be no judgments around women in prostitution, women with no recourse to public funds, women with alcohol and substance use issues and women with mental health issues. There is no 'ideal' witness, there is only the witness who is the victim of sexual violence. To drop cases because the victim is not 'ideal' is quite outrageous.

The cuts to services in the police and the CPS means that fewer cases will progress through the Criminal Justice System and there will be a need for further prioritisation of cases, meaning closing of others or less staff to investigate, or a longer time to process the investigation.

However, it's not all bad. There are many police officers and SOITs (specially trained officers) who investigate sexual violence crimes and are dedicated to ensuring the victim has the best support possible. They are disappointed and affected when a case fails to get to court or is not investigated further. There are judges who shown compassion and sensitivity in court, giving the victims the opportunity to take a break, ask questions and have support in the court. There are professionals who advocate and advise, ring, text and support throughout and after the Criminal Justice System. In short, there are people who care.

The victim does have a Right to Review, if the police close a case—which gives the victim an opportunity to ask questions about any decisions made. The Right to Review exists also if the CPS decide the case won't go to court. Again, the victim has the right to meet with the CPS and ask questions.

If we had a magic wand and could resolve some of the key issues for victims of sexual violence, if we had all the money we needed, if we had the support of all those involved in the professional and statutory agencies, our wish list would include:

- Self-defence training for young girls form primary school age.
- Self-defence training for all victims
- Shorter waiting times for victims to attend court.
- Free therapy guaranteed to be available when victim is ready.
- Financial support to move when the victim can't live in home any longer—maybe due to flashbacks, fear—with no loss of tenancy rights if in council/ housing association property.
- Lifetime restriction of movement for convicted perpetrator with reference to whereabouts of victim—if victims wishes
- Tougher jail sentences for perpetrators
- Tough jail sentences for family, friends or acquaintances who intimidate witness and their family/friends and/or who impede the criminal justice process.
- CPS to take all cases to court if the victim wants
- CPS to hold a case, if witness is unable to give evidence at the time.
- More flexibility and compassion for victims
- Respect and acknowledgment that all professionals are in

the life of a victim for a brief period in her life. How they behave and communicate, the signals and body language they exhibit will stay with them for the rest of their life.

- Gentle approach at all times: support and assistance to aid recovery, to know that not all people are perpetrators.

From our perspective, in supporting victims, there is much that needs to be improved within the Criminal Justice System, and we look forward to a time when those things have been resolved.

ABOUT ANNIE ROSE & LYNNE TOOZE

Annie Rose has been working as an ISVA (Independent sexual violence advisor) at Respond for around seven years. She previously worked for victim Support and Rape Crisis and has worked with victim/survivors of sexual violence for over fifteen years. Prior to specializing in sexual violence, she worked in the domestic violence field for Refuge and Women's Aid. She has a Diploma in Therapeutic Counselling (Humanistic) and attended the post graduate ISVA course in Worcester in 2012. She is passionate about raising awareness around the issues faced by people with a learning disability.

Lynne Tooze has been working at Respond since September 2016. She has been an ISVA since July 2010 when she was working at Eaves and then Refuge. She previously qualified with an Honours degree in Therapy and Awareness in 1993 and as an ISVA in 2013. She has worked in many different services supporting people made vulnerable by their life experiences and has worked extensively within domestic abuse services. She is passionate about sharing information around healing and life after the trauma of sexual violence.

Both Annie and Lynne have worked together for many years and started the London-wide ISVA support group which is facilitated by the SOECA partnership team. They have been proactive in raising awareness of the issues faced by people who report sexual violence to the police and take the frequently difficult journey through the criminal justice system.

Respond offers workshops and training around supporting people with a learning disability who have experienced abuse and trauma: http://respond.org.uk/

NOT WORTH REPORTING
BY JENNIFER HOLLY & LUCY ALLWRIGHT

WOMEN'S EXPERIENCES OF ALCOHOL, DRUGS & SEXUAL VIOLENCE

'Ched Evans' are two words that anyone who has been affected by rape or sexual assault probably never want to hear or see again. This high-profile case, which ended with Evans' eventual retrial and acquittal, involved a victim who had been drinking. Such a scenario is relatively common in the U.K. with figures from the Metropolitan Police showing that a third of survivors who report being raped stating that they had consumed alcohol or drugs prior to the attack[1]. As is also common in cases where the victim was under the influence of alcohol or drugs, the focus in the trial was on whether the victim had the capacity to consent to the activity that took place or whether this capacity had been impaired by her having consumed alcohol prior to the attack.

'Capacity to consent' is a complex issue when it comes to cases of rape where the victim was intoxicated at the time. The Sexual Offences Act 2003 is clear that 'spiking', i.e.

---

[1] Stanko, E. & Williams, E. (2009). Reviewing rape and rape allegations in London: What are the vulnerabilities of the victims who report to the police. In Horvath, M. & Brown, J. (Eds.), Rape: Challenging contemporary thinking (pp. 207–227). Willan Publishing, Cullompton.

administering a substance with the intent of incapacitating someone in order to sexually assault them, is an offence. The law is also unambiguous that a victim lacks the capacity to consent if she is asleep or unconscious. However, as highlighted by Judge Merfyn Hughes QC in his directions to the jury in the case of *R v Evans*, there is a significant grey area around capacity and other states of consciousness: "*[a] woman clearly does not have the capacity to make a choice if she is completely unconscious through the effects of drink and drugs, but there are various stages of consciousness, from being wide awake to dim awareness of reality. In a state of dim and drunken awareness you may, or may not, be in a condition to make choices. So you will need to consider the evidence of the complainant's state and decide these two questions: was she in a condition in which she was capable of making any choice one way or another?*"[2]

It is against this backdrop of a lack of clarity about a survivor's capacity to consent when under the influence of alcohol or drugs that, in 2012, AVA[3] conducted a small study with survivors of so-called drug-facilitated sexual assault[4]. The main aim of the research was to find out from survivors themselves what they thought about the concept of 'capacity to consent' and explore how alcohol or other drugs affected their ability to consent—or more accurately not to consent—

---

[2] R v Chedwyn Evans [2012] EWCA Crim 2559

[3] AVA (Against Violence & Abuse) is a leading charity in the U.K. working to end violence against women and girls. AVA's Stella Project was set up in 2002 to address gaps in service provision for survivors and perpetrators of domestic violence who use substances problematically, and in 2010 expanded its remit to include improving responses to survivors of sexual violence who have problems with alcohol or other drug use, as well as to survivors of violence against women who have mental health problems. This research project fell under the umbrella of the Stella Project.

[4] The full report, *Not Worth Reporting: women's experiences of alcohol, drugs and sexual violence,* can be downloaded here: https://avaproject.org.uk/wp/wp-content/uploads/2016/03/Not-worth-reporting-Full-report.pdf

when they were raped. Given the dominant and largely victim-blaming narratives around the links between alcohol and drug use and sexual violence, a second focus of the study was an exploration of the same survivors' experiences of seeking support after having been raped or sexually assaulted.

What follows is a selection of the key findings from the online questionnaire and one-to-one interviews with survivors who had consumed alcohol and/or drugs before they were raped or sexually assaulted. As a group, the survivors comprised 75 women, including one transwoman, and one man. The median age was 33 years old and 65% of the survivors were between 25 and 45 years old. Fewer survivors identified themselves as being disabled or Black or Minority Ethnic than is representative of the population, which means our analysis does not accurately reflect the complex intersection between different types of discrimination survivors might experience.

It came as no surprise to find that alcohol was the most commonly consumed substance reported by the survivors in our study: 97% of survivors had drunk alcohol and only 26% had taken other drugs. Whilst people tend to equate 'drug rape' with the victim's drink being 'spiked', various research from the U.K. and North America over the past twenty years has found that alcohol is the substance that victims have most frequently consumed before being raped or sexually assaulted (Lovett & Horvath, 2012). In another challenge to the stereotypical view of 'drug rape' as involving the victim's drink being unknowingly spiked, most survivors (80%) reported having drunk alcohol or taking drugs of their own free will. Of those who did not drink or take drugs willingly, there was a mix of some survivors having felt pressured or coerced and of others who had had their drinks tampered with.

Critical to the concept of 'capacity to consent' is understanding the various effects alcohol and other drugs have on the person who has been raped or sexually assaulted. The law in England and Wales regarding intoxication and consent has largely been concerned with the effects of alcohol and other drugs in causing physical incapacity. Broadly speaking, this study also found that the main impact of knowingly or unknowingly consuming alcohol or drugs was on survivors' bodies—namely on their ability to stay awake, to remain conscious, to move, to speak. Several survivors also noted that whilst physically able to speak, they experienced difficulties thinking clearly, for example: "*It's not that I couldn't speak, I could, but I couldn't think straight and was easily led/influenced/manipulated and therefore unable to verbally stop what was happening.*"

Some of these effects may, however, also sound familiar to many survivors who were not under the influence of alcohol or drugs as the time of being attacked. As one survivor who participated in the study highlighted, "*I felt mentally inebriated and a little bit physically unsteady. I haven't ticked more things* [on the survey], *because they weren't solely because of alcohol, but because of the combination of alcohol and the frightening situation I found myself in. I have therefore only ticked the things I felt before the assault began.*" The similarities between the effects of being intoxicated and the body's normal response to fear—and survivors' potential difficulties in distinguishing between the two—only add to the complexity of prosecuting cases of so-called drug-facilitated sexual assault.

A key finding for this study was the evidence of a clear relationship between some effects of substances and survivors' perceptions of whether they had the ability to communicate consent. Survivors who reported periods of unconsciousness, blacking out, having no memory of what happened, not being able to move or speak, feeling confused, vomiting and falling asleep were much more likely to believe that they were probably or definitely unable to communicate consent at the time of the assault. Survivors reporting this cluster of effects were also more likely to believe that their level of intoxication was linked to having been attacked. A second cluster of effects—feeling physically sensitive to touch, feeling anxious or panicky and having no sense of time—was reported by other survivors who were more likely to believe they were able to communicate consent and more likely to believe that they would have been sexually assaulted or raped regardless of what substances they had consumed.

Unsurprisingly, very few survivors in this study—only 13 out of 75—reported being sexually assaulted or raped to the police. Of those who did not report, the most frequently cited reasons were a belief that they would not access justice (44% of survivors) or that they would not be believed (42%). Sadly, the experience of the minority who did report lives up to these beliefs, with most (54%) having a negative experience. Moreover, 47% of survivors who reported to the police said that the treatment they received was worse because they had been under the influence of alcohol or drugs at the time of the assault.

The police were not the only people survivors anticipated a negative response from. Almost unanimously, the survivors in our research thought that someone who had drunk alcohol or taken drugs before an assault had less chance of being believed or supported by others than a survivor who had not consumed substances. This perception may well have contributed to the majority of survivors (59%) who thought that the assault or rape would not have happened if they had not been intoxicated stating they would have been more likely to report to the police if substances had not been involved. This was felt more keenly by the survivors who experienced the first cluster of effects of substances such as blacking out and not being able to move, who were also more likely to believe the attack was their fault.

This data paints a brutally bleak picture. Survivors of sexual violence are generally reluctant to report to the police primarily because of a fear of not being believed or being able to access justice; moreover, those survivors who were the most intoxicated at the time are caught in a trap—the substances which facilitate the assault also constitute a barrier to reporting to the police.

In an attempt to address this situation, the Crown Prosecution Service (CPS) has focused more heavily on consent, including 'capacity to consent', providing guidance for police and prosecutors on consent[5]. CPS guidance on such matters is usually good, but implementation can be inconsistent across the criminal justice system. Indeed, as a recent study observing rape trials at Newcastle Crown Court[6] found, a survivor's childhood difficulties, mental health or substance use problems are regularly used to undermine or discredit them "with no regard to the vulnerability that such experiences may have caused."[7] Furthermore, while there is a wide range of procedures in place for judges to challenge rape myths in court, the research found in some cases judges did not follow through in challenging barristers in their use of such myths as a means to discredit victims. The research also highlighted that alcohol continued to be a barrier for women in court—it was used to discredit them or as a means to make the jury question whether

---

[5] https://www.cps.gov.uk/publications/equality/vaw/what_is_con-sent_v2.pdf

[6] Ruth Durham, Rachel Lawson, Anita Lord and Vera Baird, (2016). Seeing is believing: The Northumbria Court Observers Panel. Report on 30 Rape Trials 2015–16. Available online http://www.northumbria-pcc.gov.uk/v2/wp-content/uploads/2017/02/Seeing-Is-Believing-Court-Observers-Panel-Report.pdf [accessed 30 September 2017].

[7] ibid, p. 23.

the case could be proved beyond reasonable doubt.

In turn, alcohol and drug continues to play into the victim-blaming narratives that abound both in– and outside of the courts. In 2016 a drunk young woman was raped after a night out by a man she met in a fast food restaurant. The perpetrator was caught and eventually sentenced to six years. While the case had a positive outcome, there was anger around the judge's comments in the case. In March 2017 Judge Lindsey Kushner QC said there was *"absolutely no excuse"* for sex attacks, but that men gravitated towards vulnerable women[8]. The judge further issued the warning that *"a girl who has been drinking is less likely to be believed than one who is sober at the time. I beg girls and women to have this in mind."* Instead of focussing on the choice of women to go out and drink, the emphasis should be put on the perpetrator's decision to be sexually violent. As the literature review in our study highlighted, "framing intoxication as a potential component of victim selection... has the potential to challenge victim-blaming and place scrutiny back on the perpetrator of violence and their premeditation and intent."

There is clearly much to do to address how so-called drug-facilitated sexual assault is dealt with by the criminal justice system. From our research, a primary challenge is the development of a clear framework for assessing an individual's capacity to consent in cases of sexual assault and rape. It is very difficult to draw a definitive line between capacity and incapacity by focusing on amounts consumed: alcohol and drugs affects each of us differently, and impact differently on the same person in different circumstances. However, our

---

[8] Judge criticised over warning to drunk women (11 March 2017). Guardian News. Available online: https://www.theguardian.com/society/2017/mar/11/judge-criticised-over-warning-to-drunk-women [accessed 3 October 2017].

research found that there are still possibilities for improving how drug-facilitated sexual assault cases are evidenced and prosecuted, particularly in terms of defining how certain symptoms (such as vomiting, blacking out being unable to move or speak) correlate with being incapacitated and unable to consent. When a third of survivors who report to the police have consumed drugs and alcohol prior to assault, this is clearly, at the very least, an area deserving of further research.

Beyond this, however, a much greater battle still needs to be fought. Historically, women reporting rape were trapped by the idea of the 'twin myths': "*that unchaste women were more likely to consent to intercourse and in any event, were less worthy of belief.*"[9] This is none more so than when alcohol or drugs are involved—here two sets of social and cultural norms collide: the construct of woman and the construct of intoxicated woman. Until these norms and the public opinions that they give rise to are eradicated, women will continue to be held accountable for the violence they experience. We believe that research with survivors can help fill this gap—further research on what symptoms of intoxication are associated with incapacity, awareness campaigns should include women's voices and experiences of intoxicated sexual assault; police and CPS training should include an understanding of the impact of intoxication; judicial directives can be reviewed so that rape myths connected to substances use are clearer. In turn, the way in which trauma and substances create inconsistencies in a victim's account, needs to be better understood and responded to in the investigation of sexual offences.

We can make recommendations to services and systems, but what was also clear from this research is that survivors of sexual violence are a vital resource—we can challenge societal norms

---

[9] Durham *et al*, 2016, p. 6.

through top-down changes and making recommendations, indeed we must do this. But, we can also challenge social norms together by sharing and understanding common experiences of intoxicated sexual assault and realising that when something happens to an intoxicated woman it is because *someone made a choice to harm her*. We can support each other to grasp that when we forget or are confused, this may be the substances, but it may also be a bodily reaction to violence. Change comes through knowledge and collecting women's stories gives them the tools and evidence to demand their rights and nothing less.

ABOUT LUCY ALLWRIGHT & JENNIFER HOLLY

Lucy Allwright is a project manager at AVA (Against Violence and Abuse). She has been working in the Violence Against Women and Girls sector since 2008 in a variety of frontline, training and policy roles in both the charity and public sector. She is an experienced researcher, project manager and trainer with a particular specialism in multiple disadvantage. She holds a PhD from the University of Warwick and is one of the co-founders of activist group Sisters Uncut. Her academic background makes her a skilled researcher and writer, with specialisms in the history of social policy and how it is embedded and interpreted at the national and local level. Lucy has a particular interest in improving policy through building a strong evidence base for what works. As an activist and policy maker Lucy is committed to capacity building through creating strong partnerships and widening participation to ensure broader involvement in policy making.

Having spent almost fifteen years working in the violence against women and girls sector in a wide range of roles, Jennifer Holly has acquired extensive expertise in the development and delivery of services to women affected by violence and abuse. Over the years, she has worked directly with survivors of domestic violence, rape and sexual assault, women involved in prostitution and who have been trafficked. More recently, Jennifer's roles as a researcher, trainer and organisational development specialist have focussed on improving policy, service and professionals' responses to survivors affected by mental distress and substance use problems. Jennifer has an MSc in Gender and Social Policy from the London School of Economics and is currently working towards an MSc in Psychology from the University of Derby.

Key publications include:

- Holly, J. (2017). Mapping the Maze: services for women affected by multiple disadvantage in England and Wales. London: AVA.
- Harvey, S., Mandair, S. & Holly, J. (2014). Case by case: Refuge provision in London for survivors of domestic violence who use alcohol and other drugs or have mental health problems. London: AVA.
- Holly, J. & Scalabrino, R. (2012). Treat me like a human being, like someone who matters: findings of the Stella Project Mental Health Initiative survivor consultation. London: AVA.
- Holly, J. (2012). Complicated Matters: a toolkit addressing domestic and sexual violence, substance use and mental ill-health. London: AVA.

AVA (AGAINST VIOLENCE AND ABUSE)

AVA is a leading UK charity committed to ending gender based violence and abuse. We strive to improve services for survivors through our learning, resources, consultancy and end Violence

Against Women and Girls through our policy, research and prevention work. Our particular expertise is in multiple disadvantage and children and young people. See www.avaproject.org.uk for more.

RESTORATION CIRCLE: DR NINA BURROWES

INTERVIEW BY EMILY JACOB

I have been a long admirer of Nina's and when I started working in this space, I must admit to becoming a bit of a stalker and following her around the country to Bristol and Birmingham to hear her speak. I'm delighted that she was able to find some time in her schedule to share her thoughts about the justice system.

We spoke about the concept of justice. What is it, really? It isn't the binary issue it's made out to be, it's complex and needs more sophistication and nuance. Nina raised the point, what is justice when a sibling abuses a sibling? What could it be? Justice, in her opinion, needs to be a circle, not binary, not one side against another.

For the rest of society, the concept that there is a justice system provides the feeling of security. It provides a false sense that sexual violence is under control. That the system is taking care of it.

Lawyers are supremely intelligent people, but in understanding sexual violence you also need to understand human psychology. There needs to be collaboration between law makers and other skills within the new justice circle: psychologists, social workers, therapists.

Originally, the justice system emerged from communities. Now, the justice system can feel alienated from our communities. Juries are drawn from the community, yet the people who form juries can often feel alienated from the justice system working around them too.

The idea of juries is that they make decisions that are based on the evidence. But the evidence in relation to a sexual offence is often complex and nuanced. It's unfair not to equip juries to better understand what they're hearing. It sets them up to fail. When it comes to sexual violence, we also don't equip them to not become traumatised themselves even though they may need to hear many upsetting things during the course of the trial. We don't support them enough in their role in delivering justice.

It's frustrating because if we help people see the relationship between their desire to keep their children safe from sexual crimes, would we have the same people on the jury asking, *"what was she wearing?"*

The main mechanism for identifying a sex offender is if a victim reports the crime. And yet many people feel dissuaded from doing so because they fear that a jury (and maybe also parts of the system) will not judge them fairly.

The system needs to change, but systems tend to only duplicate and reinforce themselves. Fundamental change can only come from the outside. Policy reviews and enquiries all make privilege of the things the system thinks are important.

If people are reclaiming their own justice, how are they doing it? Nina's fear is that many people are blaming themselves and living with guilt. The hope is that people are supported to find their own answers around their questions.

Justice doesn't need to mean a custodial sentence (and even when it does, it might not feel like justice). Justice can be that the victim is listened to by their family, by their work. Justice can mean that the financial impact on their life, or how the trauma has affected their parenting, is supported.

What does justice mean for those who are supporting the victims too? What is justice for the mum whose child has been abused?

Justice needs to be complex, community-based, and recognise that we have all been hurt by this crime. We couldn't currently go to court to get this kind of justice.

To make a big difference (and how sexual offences are managed in the justice system, needs a big difference), you need a big change.

In the UK, you're a complainant, you're a witness. You don't have a lawyer. In Iceland, the state prosecutes, and you get your own lawyer. This gives the victim a voice and more representation in the court room. Philosophically, you deserve to be represented. It's seems strange to pretend it's not personal. It is supremely personal.

Could we beef it up, change it, duplicate it?

Nina commented that if you're thinking about radical change then ripping it up and starting again could also be an option—even if it's unlikely. That idea took my breath away.

She observed that the existing justice system doesn't always do a great service to the abusers either. It is a life sentence, even if you get out again because of society's attitudes. You're a monster, in black and white. It traps them in this role, and their families. [Editor's note: not that it seems to matter so much if you're famous already.]

Nina asked, who is this system serving? She is drawing a blank, no-one is winning. The person who wants to get away with it, they are quite well served by it. The person who's never engaged with it, it affords them to not think about these things.

A colleague remarked recently to Nina that the justice system we're working within has been around for hundreds of years; and the general consensus is that the age of the system is a good thing. But in anything else, science, accounting, you want today's solution, not one that's hundreds of years old.

The police were not originally created to deal with sexual offences. Investigation of sexual offences needs a different type of investigation; police forces can struggle with this. For car crime, perhaps their traditional way of working is effective. But you need a fundamentally different way of thinking when investigating sexual offences.

We could be creative. We know this is a repeat offence. Why aren't we joining the dots more often? It's a serious offence, it needs to be resourced, and build an investigation around the whole picture of the offences. But it's also a high-volume offence and many officers are buckling under the pressure. If we really do want to take these offences seriously, we need to give serious resource to every report.

Nina wishes too that victims had a choice—you push start and then pretty much everything else is a passive reaction to the system. There needs to be more options. She wondered, could there be an option to not report but add some intelligence about this person.

The etymology of justice is 'the administration of the law'. This actually means that we get justice every time because the law has been administered. When we say we're not getting justice, we're substituting justice for redemption or revenge. Nina mused on restorative justice, and suggested we just leave out justice: what we want is to be restored.

The process of rebuilding and reshaping is not a bureaucratic process. What is needed is to empower people to claim (not reclaim) their restoration. Is could be as simple as inviting people to think of it in those terms, and as a community, support them.

People live with the pain that the system doesn't do as they want. Shame on us that we set it up like that. When did our thoughts about justice only ever relate to the kind of justice the system gives us? We're able to experience education, health and justice outside of those aspects that the system gives us.

We're always going to have a legal system that doesn't result in a large number of convictions because of the nature of the evidence. These are very hard cases to investigate and prosecute. Huge numbers of people won't be served. We need to put justice in its place. The much wider picture is restoration. Everyone can attempt to restore themselves after an experience of sexual violence. Very few will achieve the kind of justice our system offers. Restoration is the bigger conversation.

We can do this. It's our choice if we want to make it. No person and no system can stop you from exploring what your version of restoration could be.

Nina exclaimed that it seems unfair that she spends time training police, and judges and barristers on the traumatic brain, information that very few people already know about. But educating the jury on established aspects of science like this is not admissible in court. In other areas you get general expert evidence, but we don't currently give juries this kind of information when it comes to sexual violence. As a result, the jury hears a story that sounds like it is full of holes, and they may think the victim must be lying. Whereas it might be useful for them to know that a fragmented memory of events is very common when people have had a traumatising experience.

In closing words, Nina shared her frustration with the invasion of the complainant's life that happens in the court system. Therapy notes that are misused in the court process. The official policy is that there shouldn't be a fishing expedition into someone's past, however sometimes this is exactly what happens. School reports, medical notes, are often used. She wonders if one day we'll look back on this current part of how we apply the law and we'll wonder how people ever thought school reports and medical records were relevant in these cases.

I, for one, am looking forward to Nina's vision of a community that supports survivors to claim their restoration, and a police approach that recognises that these are multiple crimes and joins the dots.

ABOUT DR NINA BURROWES

Dr Nina Burrowes is a psychologist who helps people understand the psychology of child sexual abuse, sexual exploitation, sexual assault, rape and domestic abuse. She works closely with the police, prosecutors, barristers, and judges in the UK providing education and consultancy. She is the author of 'Responding to the challenge of rape myths in court: A guide for prosecutors' and the founder of The Consent Collective.

- Website: https://ninaburrowes.com

NEXT STEPS

AFTERWORD
BY EMILY JACOB

Back in 2014 I was supposed to be 'cured', and whilst it's true I haven't had panic attacks since, I still didn't feel like 'me'. It was when I trained to become a coach that I found that I was learning how to put 'me' back together again, and how to trust in life again.

I founded ReConnected Life in 2016 because I wanted to share my approach to the recovery journey with as many other survivors as I can. Too often we are left to our own devices to fashion our own recovery path. Which makes something that is already hard, harder.

Counselling helps treat, and can cure, our symptoms of panic, anxiety and fear. But, as I found, this wasn't enough to make me feel me.

Coaching can help us shed self-blame, shame and redefine ourselves again. And, I also found this wasn't enough either.

There is more. We also need to learn how to reconnect our minds to our bodies, so that we can reconnect ourselves to our loved ones, and ourselves to our dreams.

The ReConnected Life Experience uniquely combines knowledge of all elements through Recovery, ReDiscovery and ReConnection, enabling us to take back control of our lives and live the full & whole life we deserve.

And if you're not ready for the full programme, the

ReConnected Life Taste of Recovery will help you move beyond merely coping, one day at a time. It will help you take control of your reality, and become your own rescuer.

THE RECONNECTED LIFE COMMUNITY

The ReConnected Life Community is an online support community of survivors of rape and sexual violence.

Community is one of the most critical factors in recovery after trauma. And yet, when it comes to rape we are often isolated and alone and find it difficult to confide in anyone.

The Community won't make the pain go away. But it does help to feel supported by people who understand what you are going through, and truly care about your wellbeing.

"I never imagined an online group could provide so much community spirit, support, kindness and 'realness'."

"I love this group. Space to talk, to learn and to grow. It's so helpful!"

https://reconnected.life/community

THE RECONNECTED LIFE
TASTE OF RECOVERY

For a really long time I felt like I was having to figure out what the things were that I could be doing to make myself feel better all by myself. I don't want you to be feeling lost that way too. So, I've collected and curated the things that I think will be the MOST USEFUL for you in your recovery.

These techniques are drawn from my years of one-to-one counselling, group therapy, psychiatric treatment, my coaching training, my neuro-linguistic programming skills, and my extensive reading over all the years of my recovery path. I'm confident your recovery path can be short-circuited, and that by applying these lessons you will feel more in control and on the way to feeling much better.

Delivered as an online course, the ReConnected Life Taste of Recovery will provide you with all the essential tools so that you can begin or continue your healing journey. Through this guided self-help you will become empowered to have self-compassion, to rescue yourself from fear, and to build the foundations for your ReConnected Life.

https://reconnected.life/tasteofrecovery

THE RECONNECTED LIFE EXPERIENCE

I developed the ReConnected Life Experience to help people just like you move from a place of self-blame and disconnection; to a place where they can look forward to what the future holds, with a happy, hopeful heart.

Delivered as an online course, or through one-to-one coaching, the ReConnected Life Experience will take you from a life of self-blame, of feeling out of control, of distrusting yourself and others, of living a small and narrow life; to a life of joy, of variety, of confidence. You will look forward to what the future holds, with a happy, hopeful heart.

Rape does not need to be a life sentence. Let me guide you to your ReConnected Life.

https://reconnected.life/experience

RECONNECTED LIFE
TESTIMONIALS

TRANSFORMING LIVES IS WHY I DO WHAT I DO

"Emily is an excellent coach who is gently challenging so I don't stay stuck in my thinking. Whilst at the same time making me feel safe about sharing anything I am thinking or feeling without feeling silly. The tools she has given me help me feel confident to handle any situation. I would highly recommend Emily's programme to anyone who has suffered a trauma."

"She helped me recognize that one event in my life did not define my worth and no matter who is in my life I can be strong and stand up for myself. I am strong within myself. If you need help, talk to Emily. Sign up for her program most importantly because she understands."

"I feel so grateful for the work I'm doing with Emily which is helping me more than I can say. Xxxxxx"

"I can't recommend the sessions highly enough! Working with Emily is amazing, she just understands exactly what I need so much better than any therapist I have ever worked with. I have been dealing with this stuff for a very long time now, and really feel like I am making those big, deep changes that are sustainable. Her way of working is so gentle yet so supportive and empowering, encouraging me to take ownership of myself and my responses to the world. She has totally got my back through this, and that is exactly what I need right now. All of you do deserve this course, so do go ahead and take advantage of these offers. You are worth it."

"I contacted Emily for help when I realised that events from 23 years ago were still affecting me. However, I had no idea that her coaching program would be so transformational, I just thought she'd help me stop triggering myself. With her support, I found out, for the first time in my life, who I really am. I know how to put boundaries in place so I don't feel that I'm compromising myself or giving myself away. I've learnt skills and strategies to prevent the overwhelm and I'm a far, far happier person. She's taught me to love and accept who I am, and that's life-changing. I'm now ready to take on the world. Thank you."

"I have just completed Emily's 1:1 programme and I URGE you to look into it if you are suffering as I was. I couldn't look in a mirror—now I'm comfortable making videos. I felt shame and depression on a regular basis, now I enjoy going out with friends regularly and feel so positive about my life and relationships. I laugh more, joke more, dance more—she really has given me back my life through her amazing programme of guided meditations, helpful strategies, and coaching and challenging me in a caring way. You deserve this programme so find a way to get on it—you won't regret it. Regret is another thing you'll leave behind."

"I believe I will be eternally grateful to Emily and her work as she alone has helped me more than I feel I could have conceived possible before. Her approach and comfort offered should be awarded—what she achieves in such a short space of time is more than any other counselor has done for me previously."

ABOUT THE EDITOR

Emily Jacob is an idealist with a big dream. She dreams of a world where rape is rare, and where survivors are not shamed, and instead supported in their recovery.

After she was raped she struggled to live, wearing a façade for the rest of the world, telling everyone she was fine. In refusing to give up, and finding her own answers to how to live again, she is now on a mission to share these secrets with the countless others who need to know too.

Emily is a fierce advocate of survivors and is using her voice to break the silence and speak for survivors on issues relating to both recovery and societal attitudes and myths—she has featured as a guest blogger in Metro, Huffington Post, and Psychologies Life Labs. She featured in the Channel 5 documentary 'Raped: My Story' (Lambent Productions), and in a series of videos 'Life After Sexual Violence' for the Independent. At time of printing, she has also commented on BBC Breakfast, Radio 5 Live and Channel 5 News.

A coach and NLP master practitioner, Emily has curated the tools, techniques and resources to rape recovery which move beyond the conventional symptom-based approach and fill the gaps that she identified were needed in her own recovery path.

Emily's other career has spanned 20 years in marketing strategy and capability. She lives alone in Oxford.

15060686R00138

Printed in Great Britain
by Amazon